The New Baking

Caroline Liddell

The New Baking

LRC The Promotional Reprint Company Ltd.

Thank you
Mrs M · Heidi · Sarah · Louise · Rosalind · Laura

First published in 1988 by Bloomsbury Publishing
Limited
Copyright © 1988 by Caroline Liddell
All rights reserved

This edition published 1991 by The Promotional
Reprint Company Limited for Bookmart Limited,
Leicester, UK.

ISBN 1 85648 018 6

Designed by Fielding Rowinski
Photography by Chris Crofton
Food prepared by Sarah Bush
Printed and bound in Hong Kong

CONTENTS

FOREWORD

It is both a pleasure and a privilege to be asked to introduce this book, since the author has been a valued friend and colleague of mine for the past 20 years. During that time she helped me professionally in the early stages of my own career in cookery-writing: whenever I was baffled by a reader's complicated query, or had to call on hours of patient recipe-testing in order to present them in the simplest possible form, Caroline always came to the rescue.

There are two points I would emphasize about this book. First, here at last is someone with real solid experience who has ventured into the hitherto amateurish area of what has come to be known as 'healthy eating'. Once the wholesome properties of things 'brown' hit the headlines, it seemed like a licence to print recipes, for anyone to hurl brown flour, margarine and skimmed milk into any old recipe and make it 'healthy'. What *The New Baking* does, sensitively and imaginatively, is to offer a proper transition from the old over-sweet, high-fat, highly refined baking to a new, versatile and varied use of a whole range of ingredients that are now available on most supermarket shelves.

The other point I would make, having received thousands of letters and met countless readers at book-signings, is that the one priority for the book-buying public is that the recipes should *work*. Through her long and varied experience, the author of this book certainly knows how to test, write and present recipes that do just that. Happy baking!

Delia Smith

INTRODUCTION

Introduction

Times change, and so does our diet along with our life style. But it can still come as something of a shock when you actually register the degree of change. Shock is what I feel when I look back on what I thought of as the 'heavenly' Sunday teas of my youth: white bread sandwiches with meat paste filling to start, followed by tinned mandarin oranges and evaporated milk, and a Victoria sandwich with butter cream icing inside and out and topped with glacé cherries and angelica. I could not eat that now if I tried, so what has changed? Today I can see that such a meal consists of all the 'wrong' things: it is high in saturated fats, sugar and carbohydrate and comparatively low in vitamins, minerals and fibre – and definitely the wrong eating pattern to establish in a child! These days, I know enough about diet to say that what the Sunday tea of my youth *should* have consisted of was wholemeal bread sandwiches, fresh fruit salad with yogurt and a slice of homemade, wholemeal fruit cake. Most people would now agree that the latter sounds like a more sensible, balanced diet.

But our knowledge has been hard won and can seem impossible to put into action. Hard won, because never has there been so much conflicting advice on what to eat, or, rather, on what *not* to eat; and difficult to implement because expediencies of speed, convenience and economy have never seemed more pressing. Last, but not least, is the problem of getting the family to eat what is good for them. What food appears on the table is usually dictated by Father, whose ideas of perfection centre on the kind of food Mother used to make! Small wonder that the cook is often beaten back to adopt the line that meets with least resistance, and serve family favourites that do not have a lot to do with sensible eating, but are quick, easy and avoid argument.

However, things are changing. Certainly men are becoming more interested in cooking, so they can no longer remain quite so inured from any concern with the food they eat, and having sweated it out in the kitchen, they might not be quite so ready to censure!

The supermarkets now testify to a greater public awareness of diet in the types of foods on offer: lower in sugar, higher in fibre, additive-free, and so on. But this area is heavily mined. What has been done to muesli, for example, must have Doctor Max Bircher-Benner whirling in his grave. And to emblazon across the front of packets of crisps 'no preservatives or additives, high in fibre, seasoned with sea salt' or whatever shows just how far manufacturers are prepared to contort themselves in order to *appear* in tune with current food thinking.

What does come through, loud and clear, is the growing enthusiasm for cooking and the wish to eat a better, healthier diet amongst both men and women.

The area of cooking which has always been the favourite for experimentation is that of baking, but it is here that there seems to be the final hurdle to struggle over. I cannot help but feel that healthfood shops have done a considerable disservice to their cause in the baked items which they often have on sale. Brown and lumpy, these cakes and biscuits look fearfully unprepossessing, and often taste no better than they look. And I am afraid that carrot cake is well on its way to being as derisory a nod in the direction of the health-conscious as the nut cutlet is to the vegetarian. So some restoration work has to be done in this area – and that is how this book came about!

Ingredients

In the past there have been occasions when I have been involved in taste tests of one sort or another. Particularly interesting was one where identical items were baked, some with margarine, some with butter. There is no doubt that, in a direct comparison such as this, the flavour of butter comes out on top. But outside a specially constructed tasting session there is rarely, if ever, such an opportunity for direct comparison. Also, in this particular instance, the items baked were fairly straightforward: Victoria sandwiches, sponges, shortbreads and pastries. Once you add fruits, spices and flavourings, the difference fades away. So, with this in mind, and with an eye to the fact that we could, most of us, eat considerably less saturated fat, I decided to test all of the recipes in this book using a supermarket brand of vegetable margarine, high in polyunsaturates. And it is with this philosophy that I have pressed on. Hence you will find skimmed milk used throughout the book and an emphasis on using natural yogurt and buttermilk in preference to single or double cream. It simply seems sensible to cut fat consumption in this manner wherever possible.

Brown sugars have been used exclusively. This is not because brown sugar is 'better' for you (the additional amounts of trace vitamins and minerals are negligible), but because the flavour is actually an improvement. What matters most is that *less sugar of any kind* is eaten, and where possible quantities have been cut in the recipes. One important point: I recommend sieving these darker, sticky sugars before use as they can form rock hard lumps which are not dissipated by either the making or the baking processes.

Flour

Flour is one of the most basic ingredients, and certainly one common to every recipe in this book. It is also the ingredient that demands the most detailed explanation. To understand flour it is first necessary to know something of the wheat grain. This is made up of three distinct parts, which means that the grain lends itself particularly well to the separation processes that can go on in modern milling. There is an outer layer (or husk) called the 'bran', which contributes mostly fibre to our diet, but also some minerals, protein and B vitamins. The 'germ' is the embryo, a sort of egg yolk to the grain, and therefore rich in protein, B vitamins, vitamin E and many valuable minerals. The centre, comprising some 90% of the grain, is called the 'endosperm'. This is made up mainly of starch, with some protein. When the whole grain is milled to a flour the result is *100% wholewheat* or *wholemeal flour,* so the 'whole' prefix makes sense and is a useful way of remembering what's what.

You will often see this type of flour described on the bag as being *stoneground.* This means that the grain has been ground in the traditional manner, between two huge, circular stones, rotating at slow speeds. The distance between the grinding stones is variable so you will find that different brands of flour have slightly differing textures. The slow-grind method of milling generates a lot less heat, which means that fewer of the heat-sensitive nutrients are destroyed than with the hotter, steel-rollermilled flours. So if you are particularly concerned that the flour you use should retain the maximum food value from the grain, use stoneground varieties. There are now *plain, self-raising and strong 100% flours* available.

Flours of a lower extraction rate, around the 81% to 85% mark, are obtained by sieving out some 15% to 19% of the coarser particles, mostly bran, but retaining the greater part of the wheatgerm. Since new legislation came into force in July 1986, 85% flours are referred to simply as 'brown' and should carry the extraction rate on the bag.

However, these flours can be confusing to the buyer. They do not simply call themselves 'brown' on the bag and/or figure the extraction rate writ large. In fact, they hardly ever call themselves just brown, but usually feature names like 'Golden', 'Farmhouse' and 'Country' as well, and sometimes it is quite a hunt to find an extraction rate. But this 'mid-way' flour is particularly useful. Having some of the bran removed leaves a finer flour, with little loss of food value, which is easier to use than 100% wholewheat in a lot of cases, and this is a useful way of introducing brown flour into the diet of the wary! It should be noted, though, that wherever an 85% flour is specified in a recipe in this book, it is perfectly acceptable to use an 81% flour or a flour of any extraction rate between the two.

A few wholewheat flours and all white flours are *rollermilled*. This process was first introduced in 1879 and it was when completely white flour became widely available that, according to some authorities, our dietary problems started. But it suited the millers admirably. With the oily wheatgerm removed the flour kept much better and they had the added bonus of being able to sell the wheatgerm and bran separately. These are now sold as expensive supplements to the white flour diet, but it needs to be emphasized that, consumed in their separate parts, they do not deliver the same nutritional value. To obtain the separate parts, the grain goes through a complicated graduated system of steel rollers, unlike the single stage of milling in the stoneground method. Rollermilling starts with the wheat grain being cracked open and the starchy endosperm being separated off. The process then carries on through a complex system of rolling, sifting and refining to produce a white flour which contains some 70% of the grain. If it is to be sold as wholemeal or brown flour, the appropriate amount is replaced (i.e. 30% for wholemeal, some 15% for brown).

Frequently, white flour is then bleached with chlorine. This is not solely because the public thinks white flour ought to be white (in the same way that they insist on their tinned peas being green, or their smoked kippers tobacco brown), but because this bleaching also helps mature the flour in such a way that it takes more readily to the sort of high-technology baking process that produces today's white 'bread'. Happily, if the supermarkets I frequent are anything to go by, a lot more unbleached flour is on sale and I always buy that, given the choice.

Wheat, Sultana and Cashew Bars

It is not enough for the manufacturers to point out that the nutrients which have been destroyed by the rollermilling and bleaching processes are put back into flour, and that it is further enriched by the addition of iron, calcium and some B vitamins. The fact remains that a whole lot more is removed than is ever replaced.

As the Flour Advisory Bureau points out, when you are evaluating flours the colour and texture are plain to see, but the most important constituent of flour is hidden: the gluten content. According to the quantity of gluten in a flour it can be referred to as a *strong flour* (high in gluten), or a soft, weak flour (low).

Britain is not suitable for growing the hard wheat from which strong flour is derived, although different strains of hard wheat are now being bred that can cope with our climate. In the main, hard wheats thrive in climates like that of North America where the hotter summers and colder winters mean a shorter growing season so that the grain develops proportionately less starch and more protein. In our more temperate climate, wheat has a longer growing season, allowing the starchy endosperm to go on swelling. This produces a grain of higher starch content, but comparatively low protein content, which means we make mostly soft flour.

Baking with the different flours

The fact that we have produced mostly soft flour is why the British have a strong baking tradition and one which is founded on items such as cakes, puddings, pastries and biscuits. The slightly starchier quality of our soft (low gluten) flour gives the smaller rise, softer crumb and closer texture that characterize these goods.

Strong flour, with its relatively high proportion of gluten-producing proteins, has the greatest capacity for elasticity once it is mixed with water. This enables it to entrap gas formed by yeast and expand along with it when the dough first meets the heat of the oven. Very soon after, this framework is set by the oven heat. Thus, a high-gluten flour is what is wanted for bread-making if a large volume and open texture are what is required. I say 'if' because some people prefer this sort of loaf, but sometimes moderating the gluten content by combining strong wholewheat with (soft) plain flour produces a denser loaf with a rather better flavour.

Gluten can be strengthened or weakened in various ways. It is strengthened (or toughened) by salt. This is why the presence of the correct amount of salt is important in bread, not just for the flavour. When it is left out, the dough will feel sticky as it is kneaded. Acidity from ingredients like sour milk or lemon juice strengthen gluten and thus help to bolster the rise a little in scones and puff pastry. Handling also develops gluten. This is why bread is kneaded and conversely why some doughs have to be 'rested', as in making pastry for example. Gluten is weakened by the bran and germ of wholemeal and brown flours. This is why wholemeal baking produces a lower rise and denser texture. The presence of high levels of fat and sugar will weaken gluten, so rich yeast doughs will take longer to rise and produce less volume.

Generally, the high bran content of wholewheat and brown flours means that more liquid in some shape or form needs to be added to a recipe because the bran absorbs so much moisture.

Problems arise only when gluten levels are not specified. Then the only guide is to look at the recipes the flour miller has thought most suitable to put on the bag. This will give a good idea of how best it is to be used. Recipes for cakes, puddings and biscuits will imply a soft, low-gluten flour and you should use it in recipes similar to those described. Those flours giving bread recipes are best used for just that.

Of the other flours that you may come across, malted wheat flours are the most prevalent. These are made up of brown flour (81% to 85%) and sprouted, malted wheat and rye flakes, which produces a light, crunchy loaf with a nutty malt flavour.

Other grains produce flours of a very low gluten content, for example, rye, barley, oats, maize, buckwheat (strictly a seed) and rice. These are usually used in conjunction with the higher gluten wheat flour. They can be used in a ratio of up to 50/50 non-wheat flour to wholewheat flour (preferably strong). If gluten powder is available, add 25 g (1oz) to every 225 g (8oz) non-wheat flour to make up the natural lack.

One final word: personally I never bother to sieve flour. Certainly I very much doubt the wisdom of sieving flour in order to aerate it, and I cannot see the point of going to the trouble of sieving a batch of wholewheat flour simply to be left with a sieveful of bran that is immediately dumped straight back into the bowl to join the rest!

Storage

Resist the impulse to bulk-buy wholewheat and wheatmeal flours. The presence of the oily wheatgerm makes wholewheat flour prone to spoilage much more quickly than white flour. On most bags of flour there is now a date stamp which is usually a 'best before' date. Should you overrun this date by up to four weeks, do not immediately fling it out. It may still be in a fit condition to use. Smell it, and if it smells mouldy, sour or musty, do not use it. Similarly, if the flour seems to be holding together in lumps and is no longer free-running, do not use it. Many millers say that it is best to store flour in the bag in which it is sold, in a cool, dry place. Once opened, any lidded container will do, but flour sealed in plastic will sweat. And, of course, use up the contents of one bag before starting on another and never pour the contents of a new bag onto the remains of the old. Store flours upright in their bags, wholewheat separate from white, otherwise weevils and mites attracted by the wholewheat flour will soon invade all.

A Note on other Ingredients

All eggs used in the recipes are size 4 unless otherwise stated.

Wherever honey is required I have used clear acacia honey.

Throughout the book, almond, vanilla and any other flavourings used are *natural* essences available at healthfood shops and delicatessens. Artificial flavourings should not be used.

Finally, in every recipe where it is used, carob is interchangeable with chocolate, if preferred.

Baking Methods

Cake-making

Over the years I have dealt with a fair amount of cookery correspondence and, as a result, I have come to the conclusion that in most cases unsatisfactory results occur because people fail to follow the recipe. In cake-making it is very important to weigh ingredients accurately and combine them in the manner indicated in the recipe.

Start off with the ingredients at room temperature, especially the eggs and fat. This makes the mixture slightly less likely to curdle. Even if it does curdle, it does not mean that the cake will be ruined, it simply means that the cake will have marginally less rise and a coarser crumb texture that it would take an expert to detect. Switch on the oven, check that the shelves are positioned correctly and prepare the cake tin(s) in the manner indicated in the recipe. Have all fruits washed, dried or prepared in the manner required. Most importantly, weigh and make the cake according to the instructions in the recipe. If the mixture has to be divided equally between two tins, I counterbalance one tin against the other on my pair of balance scales to make sure the division is equal. Once the cake is in the oven, set a timer immediately. About 10 minutes before the time is up take a look to see how the baking is progressing.

Testing the cake

To test when the cake is baked, first of all, look. It is slightly more difficult to judge the degree of browning with wholefood recipes but there is usually some slight shrinkage from the side of the tin. Then touch the cake in the centre: it should offer some resistance, feeling firm and a bit springy. If there is still some doubt, insert a thin metal skewer into the centre – it should come out clean although if the cake is fruited this can be difficult to judge as the sticky fruit can adhere to the skewer. Remove the cake from the oven and sit it in the tin on a wire rack to enable the air to circulate around it (condensation forms inside the base of a cooling cake if the hot cake tin is left to cool on a solid, cool surface). Let the cake settle for 5 minutes (or according to the instructions in the recipe). Slip a knife around the edge if the cake tin is not lined with greaseproof paper, then invert the cake onto the wire rack and strip off the base papers. If it is a rich fruit cake, however, it is better to store it for a few days. In this case leave all the cake papers on and when cool wrap in a neat foil parcel before storing in a tin.

Storing cakes

I have reservations about storing cakes in plastic containers. The fact that they have such an efficient seal acts to the detriment of cakes because a warm damp atmosphere builds up around the cake, encouraging the growth of moulds. I find good, old-fashioned cake tins preferable.

Pastry

I have one bee in my bonnet when it comes to pastry. Almost without exception I feel baking *tins* should be used, especially for tarts or quiches. I know a lot of kitchens contain white, crinkle-edged ceramic flan dishes and varieties of heatproof glassware, but they do not cook pastry successfully. Tin or stainless steel is needed to cook pastry through adequately. I recommend using the crinkle-edged tart tins (preferably with a removable base), or metal rings (plain or fluted), on baking sheets. The old-fashioned enamel pie plates and tins are good and there are now stainless steel pie tins on the market, which, although expensive, are excellent and will last a lifetime.

There are two critical points in the making of pastry. The first is the addition of water. It needs to be the right amount added all at once, sprinkled over the surface of the rubbed-in mix. Now, it is impossible to be specific about the amount of water to add because it depends on a number of variables such as the temperature of the kitchen and how soft the fat is, the brand of flour and how long the packet has been open and what conditions it has been stored under. When working with white flour, a reasonably safe rule of thumb is to add 1 teaspoon of water to 25 g (1 oz) flour, but wholewheat pastry needs to be just a little wetter than white, so add an extra teaspoon of water for every 50 g (2 oz) flour. 'Cut' the water into the crumb mix (this sounds strange, but it conveys the right sort of action) and as the mix begins to come together in lumps, use your fingers to draw it together to form a dough.

Transfer to a lightly floured surface and knead lightly. This action is nothing like kneading bread dough. Use the fingers to draw the edges up and into the centre, giving the dough a quarter turn to the right and working your way around gradually until it is smooth and even, all cracks kneaded out. (Note: If working with a cut piece of pastry, put the cut side uppermost before re-kneading.) Pat the dough into something resembling the final shape required – round for a round tin, oblong for making a plait.

Rolling is the next critical point. Roll away from yourself with short, sharp actions and do not press too hard or 'steam-roller' the pastry – both methods will cause it to crack around the edge. Turning the pastry frequently will ensure a good final shape with no 'maps of Australia' instead of a neat round! Try to avoid stretching the pastry at this stage. If, for example, transferring it to a tart tin, lift the pastry by folding it over the rolling pin, rather like a sheet on a clothesline. Or, fold the round in half, then in half again (so you have a quarter segment of four layers of pastry). Locate the centre point of the pastry in the centre of the tart tin, then carefully unfold. Ease the pastry into crinkles and angles. If you push it in any way, the pastry gets its own back in the oven – it will simply retreat from where you have pushed it. Prick the base of a pastry-lined tin thoroughly with a fork, this makes it much less likely to bubble up during baking. Refrigerate at this stage if you can; about half an hour is adequate.

I never use baking beans or foil to bake blind (baking a pastry case without any filling in it). It does not seem to me to be necessary and I hate the waste of foil or beans, and the necessity of storing them.

Any other important points in the preparation of pastry will be given in the individual recipes.

Bread

Bread-making is an enormously satisfying activity. If only people would try and put aside the fears they have and the idea that 'bread-making is so complicated' and 'takes forever'. Within the chapter on bread you will find one or two recipes for doughs that do take a long time to rise, but, for the most part, I have concentrated on giving recipes that achieve a good result in a fairly short time. To make this possible I have used *vitamin C tablets* in conjunction with yeast. This method of adding vitamin C to the dough enables it to develop more quickly to the state required before baking, so it cancels out the need for one of the usual stages in rising the dough, thus speeding the whole process up. Start off by baking the Vitamin C Wholewheat Bread (page 130), it will be a revelation to you, I promise. The vitamin C tablets can be purchased from chemists. The recipes all use 25-mg tablets – if only 50-mg are to be had, buy these and simply cut them in half with a sharp knife.

Yeast need not be a problem either. Most healthfood shops and some bakers sell 25-mg (1-oz) lumps of fresh yeast. Wrapped in cling film or kept loosely in a plastic bag, it will keep in the fridge for up to two weeks. It freezes well for up to 3 months and I usually wrap it in 25-g (1-oz) packets for this purpose. You can use it straight from the freezer, stirring it into the warm liquid and, when dissolved, adding it to the flour. When it gets brown around the edges or rather gooey, either through bad storage or through straightforward staleness, it is unwise to use it as it will not be at full operating capacity. I prefer working with fresh yeast but I always have a tin of *dried yeast* on hand as a back up. Dried active baking yeast comes in the form of grey granules and as a rough rule of thumb you generally use half the quantity that you would use of fresh yeast. I prefer to buy it in the vacuum-packed tins as the small quantities sold in cellophane packets seem to become stale more quickly. The good thing about using this form of dried yeast is that it clearly demonstrates just how fresh, or stale, it is by the amount and speed with which it froths when stirred into the slightly sweetened warm liquid. When ready to stir into the dry ingredients it should have a head on it rather like a badly poured glass of beer.

25 g (1 oz) fresh yeast = 15 g (½ oz) or 1 × 15-ml tablespoon dried yeast.

The third type of yeast is fairly new; it is called Easy Blend Dried Yeast. It comes in individual sealed foil packets in a box carrying a date stamp. This type of yeast can be sprinkled directly onto the dry ingredients, so that you avoid the waiting around to allow the yeast time to froth. It should not be used as a straightforward exchange for ordinary dried yeast because this type of yeast is stronger. My advice is to use it exactly as instructed on the packet.

Rye and Caraway Seed Bread

Liquid – this is usually water, or water and milk, or it can be something like beer or cider. It should be hand-hot temperature (about 38°C/100°F). A little sugar is usually added to the liquid when you are reconstituting dried yeast. This can be any form of sweetening – sugar, honey, malt or syrup.

Salt – this is an ingredient that many people are trying to cut out of their diet. I have eaten bread where little or no salt has been added and all I will say is that it is not an experience I would care to repeat. Before cutting it out of bread recipes willy-nilly, bear in mind that it does have a chemical function in the making of bread in that it acts as a useful regulator on the yeast, too much preventing it from working, too little giving a sticky and unmanageable dough.

Fats – again, almost any form of fat can be used: butter, margarine or oil. The addition of fat helps improve the keeping and eating qualities of a loaf.

Method of making bread

I rarely bother to warm the equipment and flour before starting, but in the depths of winter it is not a bad idea.

As with pastry, a critical point is the addition of liquid to the dry ingredients. This is best added all in one go, and it's impossible to say exactly how much is needed as it depends on the brand of flour, its gluten content and how long the opened packet might have been sitting around in a hot, steamy kitchen. It is best to err a little on the side of adding too much liquid, because it is my experience that somehow a dough never recovers from having too little added.

Once the dough has been mixed, it generally has to be kneaded and this is one technique that I wish I could personally show to everyone who makes bread. I was taught a crazy way at school and it took many years of exhaustion before the Flour Advisory Bureau showed me how. First of all, kneading is not done solely with the hands and arms: it is dreadfully hard work done this way. You have to use your whole body. Have the dough ready on a lightly floured surface, and stand about a foot away from the work surface. Push the dough from the centre, away from you, using the heel of the hand. Gather the top and fold into the centre. Give a quarter turn and repeat. Develop a rocking motion with the body so it is the weight of the body that pushes the dough away and very soon you will find it is the bounce of the dough that pushes you back! Use the palms and heels of your hands and avoid tearing the dough in any way (another mistake that I used to make). As you knead, the whole character of the dough will change, starting by being soft and tacky, but ending up bouncy, elastic and smooth – the consistency is very like the feel of poking a finger into a fat tum! Kneading usually takes about 10 minutes, a little longer if you are not too skilled at it.

Rising

Moisten the bowl with oil or fat and turn the ball of dough in it to coat it. Cover the bowl with cling film or seal the dough in a plastic bag. The temperature and richness of the dough will dictate how long it takes to rise and double in size. In a warm place (about 32°C/90°F), the dough will take about one hour, about two hours at room temperature (18°–21°C/65°–70°F), about four hours in a cool place. After rising, the dough is *knocked back* to squeeze out all the air bubbles produced by the multiplying yeast, and to give the bread a good, even texture.

Shaping the dough is done next. At this stage it can be plaited, or shaped into buns, or rolled and dropped into greased bread tins. To prevent the dough drying out and thus prevented from rising, it has to be covered again by being slipped into plastic bags and left to *prove*; again until roughly doubled in bulk.

Bread is usually baked in a very hot oven, around 200°C/400°F/Mark 7 to 230°C/450°F/Mark 8. When baked, the loaves should sound hollow when tapped on the base. For a crisper crust, remove the loaves from the tins and return to the switched-off oven for 5 minutes. Cool on a wire rack and try not to slice until cold.

Storage

I find that bread keeps well, loosely wrapped in a polythene bag and stored in the salad compartment of the refrigerator. My kitchen is too warm to store bread in a bin, nor is there enough work surface to accommodate one!

Equipment

Here we touch on a subject which I get quite upset about. Having spent some time working in a shop selling kitchen equipment, I am aware that many people feel that good cookery utensils are not worth spending money on, in fact the less they need spend, the better. Not surprisingly I heartily disagree! It makes no sense to me that women who are prepared to pay a considerable sum for a dress they might wear three times, roll their eyes in horror when you suggest they buy a good saucepan costing a third of the price and which will last a lifetime. I shall not bore my readers any more than to plead that spending money on good equipment, if it is well looked after, will more than repay the investment.

The most important piece of equipment for the recipes in this book is a reliable set of *weighing scales*. The old-fashioned sort are the best, with a good-sized scale pan for ingredients on one side, counterbalanced against the platform on which the weights are put. These scales are accurate when weighing small quantities, which is useful when weighing yeast, for example. With two sets of weights, one in grams, the other in ounces, you are set for life.

Once you have weighed things accurately, the fluids need taking care of – and here it is the pick of a poor bunch. I have yet to come across an accurate, unbreakable, heatproof jug that is easily read. My choice is the unglamorous, rather inaccurate plastic jug of 2-pint (1,120-ml) capacity. Mine has withstood remarkable wear and tear. For smaller fluid measurements, get the sort of container used for measuring medicines and available from chemists. To get anything like an accurate measurement in any jug or container it is necessary to put it on a flat surface and bring your eye down to the fluid level and read off the quantity – no other method will do!

All spoon measurements in the book are based on a set of *plastic measuring spoons*. The type I have are metric at one end (15 ml, 5.0 ml, 2.5 ml, 1.25 ml) and standard spoon size at the other (1 tablespoon, 1 teaspoon, ½ teaspoon, ¼ teaspoon). All spoon measurements are level unless otherwise specified.

Again, where *baking tins* are concerned, buying good quality ones is preferable. Although I say 'tins', they need not be of this material. A lot are made of aluminium, which conducts heat well, is comparatively easy to clean and does not rust. Good, heavy tinware *is* good, when it can be found; it packs a solid, uniform heat in the oven which is hard to beat.

Non-stick tins can certainly make life easier, but, having said that, I still prefer to line the base of tins at least – but I think this is just a case of old habits dying hard! All tins usually need greasing and for this I use the type of fat used in the recipe. I rarely use oil for greasing as this tends to stick and can build up a layer that is hard to remove from baking tins. I do wash my baking tins, and dry them thoroughly, and have rarely found that 'seasoning' the tins (or any other kind of equipment come to that) makes any discernible difference except perhaps for pancake pans.

If any serious amount of baking is to go on you will need a set of *plain and fluted cutters*. The metal ones are best as they are less likely to flex if pressed down on firmly. It is important to press straight down, then lift straight up. If a twisting action is used, biscuits and scones will not keep a good shape when baked.

For the rest of the kitchen equipment I recommend the following: *plastic spatulas* (rubber ones perish too quickly) are invaluable for cleaning bowls; *a good selection of bowls*, from very large down to small (they might as well be heatproof while you are about it, so you need have no fear when whisking or melting something over a saucepan of hot water); *palette knives* – choose ones that have good flexibility; *wire cooling racks* are needed aplenty, especially with biscuit-making, I find; and finally a rolling pin – this needs to be a long, uniform shape, not the sort with slim handles either end, and an operating surface of some eight inches in the centre. I am also assuming that items such as pastry brushes, wooden spoons, sieves, scissors, etc, are all ready to hand.

Kitchen Slaves

An *electric hand whisk* is useful not only for its ability to take the arm work out of whisking but for its mobility. I use mine for many jobs such as mashing potatoes, whipping cream, whisking egg whites and making mayonnaise.

A *stand mixer* (especially with a dough hook) is useful because it can be left to get on with the job whilst you grease and line a cake tin or switch on the oven. For me, it really earns its keep when doing the initial kneading of a sticky bread dough. It is very useful on occasions to have two mixer bowls.

A *food processor*'s real *forte* is for producing quantities of a uniformly fine nut meal in a way that electric coffee grinders, liquidizers and nut mills fail to do. It will do much more, of course, but for this particular thing it is unsurpassed.

Ovens

Although mass-produced, every oven definitely has a style of its own and it is necessary to get to know the quirks of your particular oven and to read any instructions, cookery book or literature that goes with it. The literature will usually give some sort of guide on shelf positions for your oven. You will learn whether it has a tendency to 'catch' in any area and if it tends to cook slightly hotter or cooler. I would dispense with oven thermometers; either the oven is working or it is not. If it is not heating to the required temperature you will know it, because it will probably be the thermostat that is at fault, and if that is the case the oven will either heat at full blast or stay ticking over at the lowest temperature.

If you have a new oven and need to get an idea of its cooking temperament, my advice would be to bake an experimental batch of scones and a Victoria sandwich. The scones should take 12 to 15 minutes at 220°C/425°F/Mark 7 and the Victoria sandwich about 25 minutes at 180°C/350°F/Mark 4, baked on shelf positions recommended by the manufacturer. Note if there is any unevenness of baking around the edge of the cakes or in any of

Honey and Lemon Sponge

21

the scones on the baking sheet(s). Also examine the base of the scones to see that they are not over-cooked. Admittedly this test is very rough and ready but it will give some idea of how the oven is performing. Another quite important thing to check is that your oven is set level. In the absence of a spirit level, the way the cake sits in the tin will tell you whether the oven and/or shelves are level. Watch out for brown marks or 'blooming' around the area where the oven door closes. This indicates that hot air is escaping from the oven and that the seal is deficient. The thermostat will probably be keeping the oven up to temperature but it will be adding unnecessary costs to your fuel bill.

At the same time as the oven is switched on, try to get into the habit of checking that the shelves are in the right position and run in and out smoothly. Arrange the tins in the oven to allow for a good circulation of air but do not let them touch the sides of the oven or each other and avoid what you know to be 'hot spots'. Once the tin(s) are installed, close the oven door firmly and set a timer, then try to avoid opening the door again for the first two-thirds of cooking time.

Some cookery books recommend putting a pan of water in the base of the oven to generate steam, in order to give a better rise for cakes and breads. In the very unscientific confines of my kitchen I have found this makes no discernible difference. I also have my doubts as to the necessity of pre-heating any oven, but I have not come across anyone who has researched this in any scientific way.

Note Owners of fan-assisted ovens can disregard most of the above! Baked goods need not be carefully distributed as the circulation of heat is improved by the fan and this also has the effect of cutting down the baking time by about one-third. Oven temperatures may also need to be set lower; you will need to consult the manufacturer's instructions.

CAKES

Sharply-Flavoured Lemon Cake

A rather unusual idea is used here. As soon as the cake comes out of the oven a glaze of lemon juice and brown sugar is poured over it. This gives the cake a fresh, sharp lemon flavour that is in no way cloying or syrupy. It works to almost equal effect if an orange or small grapefruit is used as a substitute for the lemon.

Cake
175 g (6 oz) vegetable margarine
150 g (5 oz) 85% self-raising brown flour
150 g (5 oz) light, soft brown sugar
3 eggs
3 tablespoons bran
grated rind of 1 large lemon

Glaze
juice of 1 large lemon
150 g (5 oz) dark, soft brown sugar   SERVES 6-8

Heat the oven to 180°C (350°F/Mark 4).

Grease a deep, 18-cm (7-in) round cake tin and line the base with a circle of greaseproof paper; grease the paper.

Place all the ingredients for the cake together in a mixing bowl. Stir until thoroughly combined, then beat for about 2 minutes. Transfer the mixture to the prepared tin and bake in the centre of the oven for 1 to 1¼ hours or until the cake feels springy in the centre and begins to shrink away from the side of the tin. Remove it from the oven.

Make the glaze. In a small bowl mix the squeezed lemon juice and sugar. Pour this immediately over the hot cake and leave in the tin until cold. By this time the cake will have absorbed all the glaze. Turn out and strip off the base paper before serving.

Prune and Apple Upside-Down Cake

Use a solid cake tin for this recipe, not one with a removable base.

Topping
25 g (1 oz) light, soft brown sugar
20 (about 225 g (8 oz)) ready-to-eat prunes
6 dried apple rings, soaked overnight
20 walnut halves
2 tablespoons pumpkin seeds

MAKES 10-12 SLICES

Cake
50 g (2 oz) vegetable margarine
150 g (5 oz) light, soft brown sugar
1 egg, beaten
110 g (4 oz) 85% plain brown flour
110 g (4 oz) 100% plain wholewheat flour
4 teaspoons baking powder
2 tablespoons bran flakes

Heat the oven to 180°C (350°F/Mark 4).

Liberally grease a deep, 23-cm (9-in) cake tin, especially the base. Sprinkle the sugar over the base. Drain the prunes and apple rings, reserving 150 ml (¼ pint) of the prune soaking liquor. Pit the prunes and stuff each with a walnut half. Arrange around the edge of the tin. Place the apple rings overlapping in the centre, putting a few pumpkin seeds in the centre of each ring. There should just be room for one stuffed prune in the centre!

To make the cake, cream the margarine and sugar until light and fluffy. Beat in the egg, then fold in the dry ingredients a little at a time alternately with the prune juice. Carefully spoon the mixture over the top of the fruit and smooth with the back of a spoon. Bake in the centre of the oven for 1 to 1¼ hours or until the cake feels firm in the centre and is beginning to shrink from the side of the tin. Turn out and serve warm or cold with cream or yogurt.

Whole Fruit Cake

So called because the entire orange is chopped and incorporated into the cake. The result is a mild, beautifully moist, fruity cake. Try it.

Cake
1 medium-sized, thin-skinned orange
1 teaspoon bicarbonate of soda
175 g (6 oz) light, soft brown sugar
25 g (1 oz) vegetable margarine
1 teaspoon natural vanilla essence
1 egg
110 g (4 oz) 85% plain brown flour
110 g (4 oz) 100% plain wholewheat flour
1 teaspoon baking powder
75 g (3 oz) chopped walnuts

Topping
2 tablespoons sharp-flavoured jelly marmalade
25 g (1 oz) walnuts, very finely ground

MAKES 9 OR 16 SQUARES

Heat the oven to 180°C (350°F/Mark 4).

Grease a deep, 20-cm (8-in) square baking tin.

Squeeze the juice from the orange and pour into a measuring jug. Make up to 240 ml (8 fl oz) with boiling water.

Chop the pith and peel to about the size of shop-bought chopped peel. Put it into a mixing bowl with the orange juice and water, bicarbonate of soda, sugar, margarine and vanilla.

Beat the egg until frothy and add it to the mixture followed by the flour and baking powder. Stir in the chopped walnuts. Mix thoroughly and pour into the prepared tin. Bake in the centre of the oven for 45 minutes, or until risen and firm when pressed lightly in the centre.

Remove the cake from the oven and leave to cool in the tin for 15 minutes. Turn out onto a wire rack and smooth the marmalade jelly over the surface. Dust the top with the finely ground walnuts. Leave until cold before cutting into 9 or 16 squares.

Mango and Hazelnut Roll

The flavours of hazelnut and mango complement each other very well. Dried mangoes are by no means universally obtainable but should you come across them, this recipe makes a delicious introduction. Dried apricots, although more prosaic, work almost as well.

Filling
175 g (6 oz) dried mangoes
1-2 teaspoons brown sugar
juice of ½ lemon
110 ml (4 fl oz) whipping cream
1 tablespoon yogurt

Roll
50 g (2 oz) hazelnuts
75 g (3 oz) unbleached plain white flour minus
    1 tablespoon flour
1 teaspoon baking powder
2 eggs
75 g (3 oz) light, soft brown sugar

Coating
3 tablespoons light, soft brown sugar
4 tablespoons wheatgerm

SERVES 6

Put the mangoes in a saucepan with water to cover. Bring to the boil, cover and simmer gently for 10 to 15 minutes, or until all the mango pieces are tender. Drain, reserving the liquor, then process, blend or rub the mango through a sieve to obtain a smooth purée. Add the sugar and lemon juice to the purée and thin with 2 or 3 tablespoons of the reserved liquor to give an easily spreadable purée. Cover and put aside while you make the roll.

Heat the oven to 200°C (400°F/Mark 6).

Put the hazelnuts on a baking sheet and transfer to the oven to brown for 10 minutes. Tip the nuts roasted onto a teatowel and rub with the towel to remove most of the skins.

When cool, transfer the skinned nuts to a food processor. Add the flour and baking powder. Process until the nuts have been reduced to almost the same consistency as the flour. Because of the oil in the nuts the flour will form firmish lumps. Break these down by sifting before incorporating the flour into the cake mixture.

Grease and line a Swiss roll tin, base measurement 18 × 28 cm (7 × 11 in) and liberally grease the lining paper.

Place the eggs and sugar in a large mixing bowl. Whisk with an electric mixer for about 5 minutes or until the mixture is thick enough to hold a trail and has a thick, fluffy texture. Using a metal spoon, carefully fold in the hazelnut and flour mixture. Spread the mixture evenly in the prepared tin and bake in the centre of the oven for 7 to 10 minutes.

While the cake is baking, place a piece of greaseproof paper on the work surface. Combine the brown sugar and wheatgerm and sprinkle this mixture evenly over the paper.

When the roll is cooked it will be tinged brown on top, and feel firm in the centre. Turn the cake out onto the greaseproof sheet and strip off the lining paper. Roll up from one shorter edge, rolling the greaseproof paper into the roll as you go. Leave rolled up until cool. Unroll carefully and spread with the mango purée. Whip the cream and yogurt and spread over the mango. Roll up, trim off each end of the roll, sprinkle with a little of the coating mixture and chill until ready to serve.

Peanut Butter and Carob Cake

An unusual combination of flavours and a different method of making a sponge and frosting produce a dark, moist sponge cake with a slightly crunchy frosting. Delicious even if, like me, you are not a great peanut butter lover.

Cake

100 g (4 oz) crunchy peanut butter
2 tablespoons carob powder
110 ml (4 fl oz) buttermilk
110 ml (4 fl oz) water
1 teaspoon natural vanilla essence
175 g (6 oz) light, soft brown sugar
150 g (5 oz) 85% plain brown flour
½ teaspoon bicarbonate of soda
1 egg, beaten

Frosting

225 g (8 oz) Demerara sugar
110 g (4 oz) vegetable margarine
2 rounded tablespoons carob powder
2 tablespoons buttermilk

Filling

2-3 tablespoons crunchy peanut butter

To finish

3 tablespoons skinned, chopped peanuts

SERVES 6-8

Heat the oven to 180°C (350°F/Mark 4).

Grease two shallow, 18-cm (7-in) sandwich tins.

Put the first five ingredients in a saucepan and bring to the boil. Meanwhile mix the sugar, flour and bicarbonate of soda in another bowl. Pour the boiling liquid over the dry ingredients, stir until mixed, then add the beaten egg. Mix thoroughly and divide equally between the two prepared tins. Level the mixture with the back of a spoon and bake in the centre of the oven for about 30 minutes or until the cakes feel firm in the centre and shrink slightly from the side of the tin. Turn out and leave upside down on a wire rack to cool.

Meanwhile, prepare the frosting. Powder the sugar in a liquidizer goblet, a small batch at a time, feeding the sugar through the hole in the lid onto the whirling blades. (It is not possible to do this with a food processor.) Transfer the powdered sugar to a bowl. Put the remaining ingredients in a saucepan and bring to the boil. Pour onto the powdered sugar and mix well. Allow to cool, then leave in the refrigerator until needed.

Thinly spread the base of one sponge with peanut butter; spread the other with some of the thickened frosting. Join the two spread surfaces and coat the whole cake with frosting. Scatter the top with chopped nuts. Chill until ready to serve. Cut into small slices (it is quite rich) and serve with forks.

Apple and Juniper Cake

A dark, moist cake with a lovely, rather autumny flavour. It can be served hot (delicious with soured cream) or eaten cold. I never peel anything unless I really have to; the apples in this recipe therefore have their skins left on. Peel them if you prefer.

Cake
2 medium-sized cooking apples
330 ml (12 fl oz) vegetable oil
350 g (12 oz) light, soft brown sugar
3 eggs
350 g (12 oz) 85% plain brown flour
1 tablespoon bicarbonate of soda
grated rind of 1 orange
10 crushed juniper berries
½ teaspoon freshly grated nutmeg

Gin and juniper glaze
50 g (2 oz) vegetable margarine
6 tablespoons light, soft brown sugar
4 tablespoons apple juice
2 tablespoons orange juice
6 crushed juniper berries
2-3 tablespoons gin
2 tablespoons single cream

MAKES 10-12 SLICES

Heat the oven to 170°C (325°F/Mark 3).

Grease a deep, 25.5-cm (10-in) round cake tin. Line the base with a circle of greaseproof paper; grease the paper.

Quarter and core the apples and chop into roughly 0.5-cm (¼-in) dice.

In a large mixing bowl, beat together the oil and sugar until thickened and opaque. It will take about 5 minutes using a hand mixer. Gradually beat in the eggs, one at a time, beating well between each addition. Stir in the remaining ingredients and, last of all, the apples. When thoroughly mixed, spoon into the prepared cake tin. Bake in the centre of the oven for 1¼ to 1½ hours, or until the cake feels firm in the centre and shows signs of shrinkage from the side of the tin. Cool for 10 minutes in the tin.

Meanwhile, prepare the glaze by heating the margarine and sugar together in a small saucepan until melted. Add the apple and orange juices and the crushed juniper. Bring to the boil and boil briskly for about 4 minutes or until the glaze has a syrupy consistency. Remove the pan from the heat and stir in the gin. Leave until just warm, stir in the cream. (Taste and add more gin, if liked!) Pour over the cake. Serve hot or cold.

Nut and Meringue Squares

You can use any type of nut for this recipe, except peanuts.

Base	*Topping*
225 g (8 oz) porridge oats	3 egg whites
110 g (4 oz) light, soft brown sugar	75 g (3 oz) light, soft brown sugar
25 g (1 oz) bran	110 g (4 oz) mixed chopped nuts (e.g., walnuts,
110 g (4 oz) vegetable margarine	hazelnuts, Brazils, almonds, cashews)
3 tablespoons vegetable oil	
3 egg yolks	MAKES 12

Heat the oven to 180°C (350°F/Mark 4).

Grease a shallow, rectangular tin, 27 × 16.5 × 3 cm (10½ × 6½ ×1¼ in).

Combine the oats, sugar and bran in a bowl. Melt the margarine in a small saucepan and pour onto the dry ingredients, followed by the oil and egg yolks. Mix thoroughly and press the mixture into the prepared tin. Bake in the centre of the oven for 12 to 15 minutes.

Meanwhile, whisk the egg whites until stiff but not dry; gradually whisk in the sugar until the meringue will hold firm, high peaks. When the 15 minutes is up remove the tin from the oven and quickly spread the meringue on top. Strew thickly with the nuts. Reduce the oven temperature to 150°C (300°F/Mark2) and return the cake to the centre of the oven to bake for a further 30 minutes. Leave until warm before cutting into 12 squares.

Sharp Seedy Honey Squares

Cake	*Topping*
50 g (2 oz) vegetable margarine	2 tablespoons lemon juice
5 tablespoons clear honey	3 tablespoons clear honey
2 eggs	
rind and juice of 1½ lemons	
75 g (3 oz) sesame seeds	
75 g (3 oz) 85% plain brown flour	
75 g (3 oz) 100% plain wholewheat flour	
2 teaspoons baking powder	
2 tablespoons skimmed milk powder	MAKES 16

Heat the oven to 180°C (350°F/Mark 4).

Grease a deep, 20-cm (8-in) square baking tin. Line base and sides with greaseproof paper; grease the paper.

In a mixing bowl beat the margarine and honey together until thoroughly combined. Beat in the eggs one at a time and, still beating, incorporate the lemon rind and juice and the sesame seeds. Combine the remaining dry ingredients and, using a large metal spoon, fold into the egg mixture. Pour into the prepared tin and bake in the centre of the oven for about 45 minutes, or until a thin metal skewer inserted in the centre of the cake comes out clean.

Remove the cake from the oven and prick it all over with a skewer. Combine the lemon juice and honey and pour over the cake. Leave until barely warm before cutting into 16 5-cm (2-in) squares. These are best eaten fresh but they will keep for up to four days in an airtight container.

Orangey Shredded Wheat Cake

People see the Greek-style kadaife *topping on this and immediately assume the cake is going to be syrupy and sweet. There is always a delighted reaction after the first orangey mouthful.*

Cake
50 g (2 oz) vegetable margarine
75 g (3 oz) light, soft brown sugar
2 eggs, separated
rind and juice of 2 oranges
150 g (5 oz) 85% plain brown flour
1 teaspoon baking powder
75 g (3 oz) ground hazelnuts
1 Shredded Wheat biscuit, crumbled

Topping
3 tablespoons clear honey
2 tablespoons orange juice
1 crumbled Shredded Wheat biscuit
25 g (1 oz) toasted, chopped hazelnuts

MAKES 16 SQUARES

Heat the oven to 180°C (350°F/Mark 4).
Grease a deep, 20-cm (8-in) square cake tin.
In a mixing bowl, cream the margarine and sugar together until light and fluffy. Beat in the egg yolks, one at a time, followed by the orange rind. Add the flour and baking powder in small amounts, alternately with the juice of the oranges. Stir in the crumbled Shredded Wheat. Finally, whisk the egg whites until stiff but not dry and fold into the cake mixture carefully using a large metal spoon. Transfer the mixture to the prepared tin and bake in the centre of the oven for about 40 minutes until the cake is risen, golden brown and firm to the touch in the centre.
Remove the cake from the tin and prepare the topping by combining all the ingredients together in a bowl. Fork the mixture over the top of the hot cake and leave until cold before cutting into squares with a sharp knife.

Fresh Blackberry and Spice Cake

A good recipe for using up the rather squidgy substrata you find at the bottom of the container after a blackberry expedition – exactly how and why this recipe came about, in fact!

Cake
150 g (5 oz) vegetable margarine
175 g (6 oz) light, soft brown sugar
4 eggs
225 g (8 oz) 85% plain brown flour
1 teaspoon ground cinnamon
1/2 teaspoon freshly grated nutmeg
1/2 teaspoon ground allspice
170 ml (6 fl oz) buttermilk or natural yogurt
1 teaspoon bicarbonate of soda
175 g (6 oz) fresh blackberries

Topping
3 tablespoons bramble jelly
175 g (6 oz) fresh blackberries
110 ml (4 fl oz) double cream
2 tablespoons natural yogurt or buttermilk   MAKES 10 TO 12 SLICES

Heat the oven to 180°C (350°F/Mark 4).

Grease a loaf tin, base measurement 20 × 10 cm (8 × 4 in) and 7 cm (2¾ in) high. Line the base with a greaseproof paper; grease the paper.

In a large bowl cream the margarine and sugar together until lightened in colour. In a separate bowl beat the eggs until frothy. Add the egg to the creamed mixture, a little at a time, beating well between each addition. As soon as the mixture looks as though it has taken in as much egg as it can and is on the point of curdling, combine the flour and spices and add a spoonful at a time, alternately with the remaining egg. Whisk together the buttermilk and bicarbonate of soda with a fork and incorporate them into the cake mixture. Finally, fold in the blackberries. Transfer the mixture to the prepared tin and bake in the centre of the oven for 1 hour 15 minutes. Test by inserting a thin metal skewer; it should come out clean. Leave the cake to cool in the tin before turning out onto a wire rack.

Make the topping. Melt the jelly in a small saucepan. Remove the pan from the heat and fold in the blackberries. Leave on one side until cold.

Meanwhile beat the cream and yogurt together until the cream will hold a firm shape. Transfer to a piping bag fitted with a rosette nozzle and pipe a border of cream around the top of the cake. Pour the cooled blackberries onto the cake and spread carefully up to the edge of the cream. Chill until ready to serve. (A 'fork' cake I think!)

Cinnamon and Almond Crumb Cake

The cinnamon-flavoured crumble runs like a seam through the centre of this cake and is used as a topping.

Crumble

110 g (4 oz) Muscovado sugar
50 g (2 oz) unblanched chopped almonds
40 g (1½ oz) 100% plain wholewheat flour
25 g (1 oz) vegetable margarine
3 teaspoons cinnamon

Cake

100 g (4 oz) vegetable margarine
110 g (4 oz) light, soft brown sugar
2 eggs
75 g (3 oz) 100% plain wholewheat flour
75 g (3 oz) 85% plain brown flour
2 teaspoons baking powder
2 tablespoons milk

SERVES 6-8

Heat the oven to 170°C (325°F/Mark 3).

Grease a deep, 18-cm (7-in) round cake tin. Line the base and sides with greaseproof paper; grease the paper.

Prepare the crumble mixture by combining all the ingredients together in a bowl, then rub in the margarine to give a crumbly texture.

In a separate bowl, cream the margarine and sugar. Gradually add the eggs, one at a time, beating well between each addition. Fold in the dry ingredients and mix to a soft dropping consistency with milk. Spoon half the mixture into the prepared tin and sprinkle half the crumble mixture evenly over the surface. Top with the remaining mixture and crumble and bake in the centre of the oven for about 1 hour 30 minutes. When cooked the cake should feel firm in the centre and show signs of shrinkage from the side of the tin. Leave until just warm before removing from the tin and greaseproof paper.

Fresh Orange and Carob Cake

One absolute essential for this recipe is a sharp knife, or you will be driven mad trying to cut even, paper-thin slices of orange. It is also necessary for serving the cake! A tip for food processor owners: process the nuts and carob together until fine, to avoid the more laborious grating.

150 g (5 oz) light, soft brown sugar
2 thin-skinned oranges
110 g (4 oz) vegetable margarine
2 eggs
175 g (6 oz) 85% self-raising brown flour
50 g (2 oz) grated carob bar or plain chocolate
75 g (3 oz) ground hazelnuts
3 tablespoons orange and lime jelly marmalade   SERVES 6-8

Heat the oven to 180°C (350°F/Mark 4).

Using your fingers, liberally grease an 18- to 19-cm (7- to 7½-in) deep, round cake tin, making sure the base is especially well coated. Sprinkle in 25 g (1 oz) of the sugar.

Scrub the oranges, dry and slice one and half of the other as thinly as possible. Arrange the most perfect slices in overlapping concentric circles in the base.

Put the margarine and remaining sugar in a mixing bowl. Grate in the rind of the remaining half-orange; squeeze the juice and reserve. Cream the butter and sugar mixture. Beat in the eggs, one at a time, beating well between each addition. Fold in the flour, followed by the orange juice, then the carob or chocolate and nuts. Spoon half the mixture into the tin and tap the tin on the work surface to settle and even out the mixture. Lay the remaining oranges in a similar pattern over the surface and top with the remaining mixture. Bake in the centre of the oven for 1 to 1¼ hours or until the cake shows signs of shrinkage and a skewer, inserted in the centre, comes out clean. Leave for a few minutes before turning out. Meanwhile gently melt the marmalade. Slip a knife around the edge of the cake and turn out onto a wire rack. Coat the surface with the glaze and leave until cold.

Carrot and Caraway Buns

These lovely, light, moist buns with a fresh-tasting orange and cream cheese filling are beautifully easy to make.

Buns
175 g (6 oz) carrots, freshly grated
175 g (6 oz) dark, soft brown sugar
200 ml (7 fl oz) sunflower oil
2 eggs, beaten
175 g (6 oz) 100% plain wholewheat flour
50 g (2 oz) ground almonds
50 g (2 oz) wheatgerm
2 teaspoons caraway seeds
1 teaspoon bicarbonate of soda
rind of 1 orange

Filling
flesh of 1 orange
225 g (8 oz) fromage frais
1-2 tablespoons honey   MAKES 16

Heat the oven to 170°C (325°F/Mark 3).

Place the paper cake cases in bun tins.

Put the grated carrots in a large bowl then stir in the ingredients one by one, in the order given above. Divide the mixture equally between the paper cake cases and bake in the centre of the oven for 30 minutes, or until they are risen and firm to the touch in the centre. (You may need to do this in two batches.) Remove and leave on a wire rack until cold.

Prepare the filling by peeling, segmenting and chopping the orange, discarding all the pips. Transfer to a bowl and stir in the fromage frais and honey to taste.

Cut a 'V' shape across the centre of each bun – approximately 2 cm (¾ in) wide and deep. Lift out the wedge of cake, spoon some filling into the channel and place the wedge back on top. Chill until ready to serve.

Gooseberry Cake Flavoured with Rosemary

Ideally, these cakes should be baked in sandwich tins with removable bases, but these are fairly hard to come by, so I have given a slightly different technique for lining the usual solid tins which will enable the cakes to be lifted from them when baked. If you have the removable-base variety, simply line with a base paper only, as usual.

Cake
110 g (4 oz) vegetable margarine
110 g (4 oz) light, soft brown sugar
2 eggs, beaten
110 g (4 oz) 85% plain brown flour
2 tablespoons wheatgerm
1½ teaspoons baking powder
½ teaspoon ground rosemary
450 g (1 lb) gooseberries, topped and tailed

Filling and topping
4 tablespoons soured cream or *fromage frais* or
curd cheese mixed with a little milk to give a
spreadable consistency
2 tablespoons Demerara sugar

SERVES 6-8

Heat the oven to 170°C (325°F/Mark 3).

You will need to remove one of the baked cakes from its tin without inverting it on to a wire rack. The following method of preparing the tins will enable you to do that. Grease two 16-cm (7-in) round sandwich tins. Cut four strips of greaseproof paper 23 × 5 cm (9 × 2 in). Fold each strip in half lengthwise. Arrange two strips cross-wise in the base of each tin, the top edges coming above the tops of the tins. Grease the strips. Now put a base paper in each tin in the usual way. Grease this also.

In a bowl, beat the margarine and sugar together until paler in colour. Gradually beat in the eggs, a little at a time, beating well between each addition. Fold in the flour, wheatgerm, baking powder and rosemary. Divide the mixture equally between the two prepared tins and level it with the back of a spoon. Dot gooseberries regularly over the surface without pressing them into the cake mix in any way.

Bake in the centre of the oven for 50 minutes, or until the cakes begin to shrink from the sides of the tins. Leave to cool in the tins for 10 minutes. Keeping the better looking cake for the top, invert the other onto a wire rack and strip off the base papers. Lift the top cake from the tin using the strips of greaseproof paper and leave to cool right side up. When still just warm, spread the base cake with soured cream or fromage frais and sprinkle with 1 tablespoon of Demerara sugar. Strip the base papers off the better round and place on top. Sprinkle the surface with the remaining Demerara sugar. Serve with additional soured cream, if liked.

Poppy Seed and Buttermilk Cake

Remember to start this recipe the night before by soaking the poppy seeds in buttermilk. It is worth it; the cake is very good.

240 ml (8 fl oz) buttermilk
50 g (2 oz) poppy seeds
225 g (8 oz) vegetable margarine
250 g (9 oz) light, soft brown sugar
5 eggs, separated
275 g (10 oz) 85% brown plain flour
25 g (1 oz) wheatgerm
2 teaspoons baking powder
1 teaspoon bicarbonate of soda
1 teaspoon natural vanilla essence
50 g (2 oz) Muscovado sugar
1 teaspoon cinnamon
50 g (2 oz) sunflower seeds

SERVES 8-10

Measure the buttermilk into a bowl and stir in the poppy seeds. Cover the bowl with cling film and leave overnight in the refrigerator. The following day remove the bowl first thing to allow the contents to come up to room temperature before incorporating into the cake.

Heat the oven to 180°C (350°F/Mark 4).

Grease a deep, 23-cm (9-in) round cake tin. Line the base and sides with greaseproof paper; grease the paper.

In a large mixing bowl cream the margarine and sugar. Gradually beat in the egg yolks, one at a time. Combine the flour, wheatgerm, baking powder and bicarbonate of soda and add to the creamed mixture alternately with the poppy seed and buttermilk mixture. Whisk the egg whites until stiff, but not dry. Stir 3 heaped tablespoons into the mixture, then fold in the remainder using a large metal spoon. Pour half the mixture into the prepared tin. Combine the Muscovado sugar and cinnamon and sprinkle over the mixture in the tin. Spoon in the remaining mixture and sprinkle the surface with the sunflower seeds.

Bake in the centre of the oven for about 1 hour 30 minutes, or until the cake is well risen and a skewer inserted in the centre comes out clean. Leave to cool in the tin before removing. Store, wrapped in the greaseproof paper, until ready to serve.

Banana Cake with Sesame Seed Crunch

Banana cakes have tended to be loaves in the past so I have attempted to make a change here by making this a sandwich cake of not quite so dense a mixture. For the filling, I have sharpened the cream by mixing it with some yogurt, which makes a good combination with the sweet cake and sesame brittle.

Cake

110 g (4 oz) vegetable margarine
250 g (9 oz) light, soft brown sugar
2 eggs
2 ripe bananas
4 tablespoons buttermilk or yogurt
150 g (5 oz) 100% plain wholewheat flour
150 g (5 oz) 85% plain brown flour
25 g (1 oz) wheatgerm
½ teaspoon baking powder
¾ teaspoon bicrabonate of soda

Filling

75 g (3 oz) light, soft brown sugar
50 g (2 oz) sesame seeds
150 ml (¼ pint) double cream
3 tablespoons yogurt

SERVES 10

Heat the oven to 180°C (350°F/Mark 4).

Grease two 20-cm (8-in) round sandwich tins. Line the bases with circles of greaseproof paper; grease the papers,

In a mixing bowl beat the margarine and sugar together until pale. Break the eggs into a separate bowl, beat until frothy, then add to the creamed mixture, a little at a time, beating well between each addition. Mash the bananas in a bowl and beat in the buttermilk or yogurt. Combine the remaining dry ingredients. Now add the banana and dry ingredients alternately to the mixture, again beating after each addition. Pour an equal quantity of mixture into each of the two prepared tins and bake in the centre of the oven for about 50 minutes or until the cakes have clearly shrunk from the sides of the tins and feel firm in the centre. Turn out onto a wire rack, strip off the base papers and leave to cool.

Prepare the sesame seed crunch. Put the sugar into a medium-sized saucepan and cook over a moderate heat. As soon as the sugar begins to melt and bubble in patches, stir with a wooden spoon until it has all melted and the sugar granules have gone. It should look slightly darker than honey. Quickly remove the pan from the heat and stir in the sesame seeds. Pat the mixture flat onto a baking sheet and leave until cold. Break it up by tapping with a rolling pin. Save ten pieces of brittle about the size of a fingernail for decoration, then crush the rest a little finer, about peppercorn size.

Combine the cream and yogurt and beat until the cream will hold a soft shape. Use three-quarters of it to spread on the bases of both cakes. Sprinkle both with half the sesame brittle. Sandwich the two halves together. Use the remaining cream to spoon (or pipe) 10 blobs of cream around the top edge. Sprinkle the centre of the cake with the remaining brittle and top each cream blob with a reserved piece of brittle. Chill until ready to serve. Keeps, looking respectable for about three days if kept chilled; its excellent eating quality will not be affected for up to six days.

Fig and Fresh Orange Cake

The runniness of the mixture for this cake can seem alarming, especially in view of all the fruit it has to support; but it works! It is a cake which improves on keeping, but not for more than a week.

175 g (6 oz) dried figs
1 large orange
6 tablespoons clear honey
75 g (3 oz) light, soft brown sugar
175 ml (6 fl oz) vegetable oil
2 eggs
225 g (8 oz) 100% plain wholewheat flour
1½ teaspoons baking powder
50 g (2 oz) wheatgerm   SERVES 6-8

Heat the oven to 170°C (325°F/Mark 3).

Grease a deep, 18- or 19-cm (7- or 7½-in) round cake tin. Line the base and sides with greaseproof paper; grease the paper.

Using a pair of scissors, snip the figs into small pieces into a bowl, discarding the central bits of hard stalk in each. Grate in the orange rind, then peel and divide the orange into its separate segments, stripping off as much of the white pith as you can. Still using the scissors, snip the orange segments into the bowl, discarding any pips you come across. Mix and set aside whilst making the cake.

Measure the honey into a mixing bowl and add the sugar, oil, eggs, 2 tablespoons water and half the measured flour. Mix together, then beat for a minute until the mixture is smooth and shiny. Stir in the remaining flour, baking powder and wheatgerm, and, finally, all but 2 tablespoons of the prepared fruit. Spoon the mixture into the prepared tin and sprinkle the remaining fruit over the surface.

Bake in the centre of the oven for 1 hour 15 minutes. Lay a sheet of foil over the top of the tin and continue baking for a further 30 to 45 minutes. When cooked the cake should feel firm to the touch and show signs of shrinkage away from the side of the tin.

Remove the cake from the oven and leave to cool in the tin for 15 minutes. If the cake is to be kept before eating, store it still wrapped with the greaseproof paper.

Exotic Fruit Cake

This makes a good cake with a definitely different flavour. I know the list of ingredients looks daunting, but if you have everything weighed, chopped and ready before starting, the cake almost makes itself.

200 g (7 oz) 85% plain brown flour
200 g (7 oz) 100% plain wholewheat flour
3 teaspoons baking powder
½ teaspoon bicarbonate of soda
½ teaspoon freshly grated nutmeg
¼ teaspoon ground cloves
½ teaspoon mace
2 teaspoons cinnamon
175 g (6 oz) dried figs, chopped
peel of 1 orange, chopped
peel of ½ grapefruit, chopped
110 g (4 oz) fresh dates, chopped
110 g (4 oz) Brazil nuts, sliced
150 g (5 oz) dried pineapple, chopped
50 g (2 oz) dried mango, snipped into slivers
3 large ripe bananas
275 g (10 oz) vegetable margarine
200 g (7 oz) light, soft brown sugar
2 teaspoons grated, fresh ginger
4 eggs
50 g (2 oz) unblanched slivered almonds

MAKES ABOUT 20 SLICES

Heat the oven to 150°C (300°F/Mark 2).

Grease and line the base and sides of a deep, 25.5-cm (10-in) round cake tin with greaseproof paper; grease the paper.

Combine the flours, raising agents and spices in a bowl. In a separate bowl combine the chopped figs, orange and grapefruit peel, dates, Brazil nuts, pineapple and mango slivers. Take a couple of heaped tablespoons of the measured dry ingredients, and combine with the chopped fruit and nuts. Peel the bananas and mash to a pulp. In a large bowl cream the margarine, sugar and ginger until paler in colour. Add the eggs, one at a time, beating well between each addition. Add the flour in several batches alternating with several additions of banana pulp. Finally fold in the fruit and nuts. When thoroughly mixed, transfer to the prepared tin. Sprinkle with the slivered almonds and bake in the centre of the oven for 3 hours or until a thin metal skewer inserted in the centre of the cake comes out clean. Remove the cake from the oven and leave to cool in the tin. Store, wrapped in the cake lining papers in an airtight container for several days before cutting.

Date and Walnut Cakes with Toffee Topping

These will keep for about four days but are best eaten fresh. Work quickly once the topping mixture has boiled, dipping the top of each cake first in the toffee, then in the chopped walnuts If you don't, the topping sets and the walnuts will not stick.

Cake
225 g (8 oz) plain 100% wholewheat flour
1 teaspoon baking powder
110 g (4 oz) light, soft brown sugar
110 g (4 oz) vegetable margarine
110 g (4 oz) chopped, pitted dates
75 g (3 oz) chopped walnuts
2 eggs, beaten
1-2 tablespoons milk

Topping
75 g (3 oz) dark, soft brown sugar
40 g (1½ oz) vegetable margarine
2 tablespoons single cream
50 g (2 oz) chopped walnuts

MAKES 16

Heat the oven to 180°C (350°F/Mark 4).

Place 16 paper cake cases in bun tins.

Combine the flour, baking powder and sugar in a large bowl. Rub in the fat until the mixture resembles breadcrumbs. Stir in the dates and walnuts, followed by the beaten eggs and mix to a soft dropping consistency, adding a little milk if necessary. Divide the mixture evenly between the cake cases. Bake in the centre of the oven for 30 minutes or until risen and firm to the touch. Remove from the oven and leave the cakes to cool on a wire rack.

When cold prepare the topping by combining the sugar, margarine and cream together in a small saucepan. Bring to the boil, stirring; boil gently for 3 minutes until slightly darkened in colour. Spoon a little topping quickly over each cake and turn them, head-first, in the chopped walnuts. Leave until cool and firm before eating.

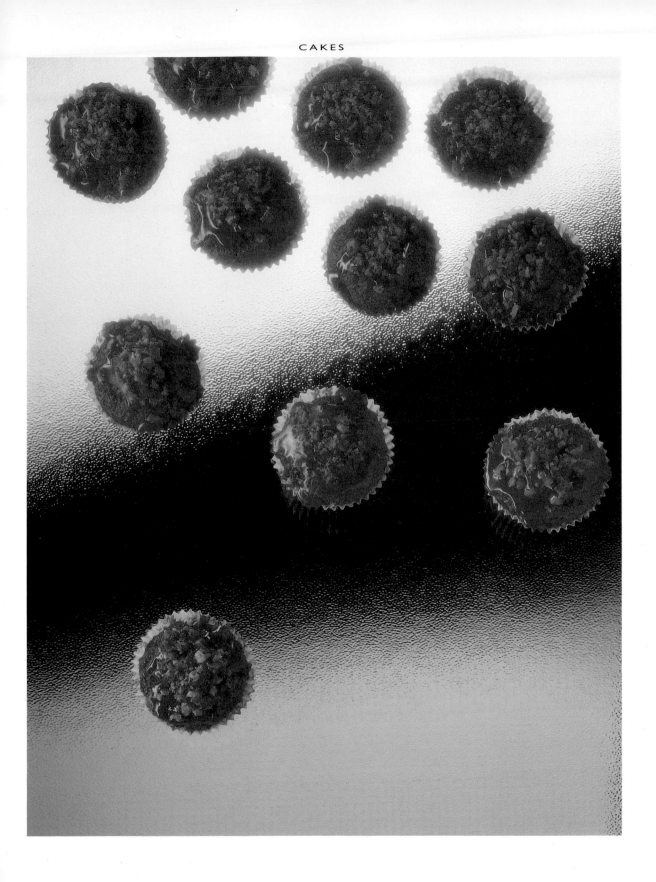

Lemon, Ginger and Pear Cake

This is one of my own personal favourites. I can only recommend that you try it. Pear and Apple Spread is widely available from healthfood shops and some supermarkets. It is simply the concentrated juice of apples and pears with no additives at all.

Cake
175 g (6 oz) vegetable margarine
175 g (6 oz) light, soft brown sugar
3 eggs
2 tablespoons clear honey
1 tablespoon molasses or black treacle
2 tablespoons grated, fresh ginger
grated rind of 1 lemon
225 g (8 oz) 85% self-raising brown flour
2 tablespoons milk
2 ripe pears

Lemony glaze
110 g (4 oz) Pear and Apple Spread
1 tablespoon lemon juice
2 tablespoons Demerara sugar

MAKES 15 SQUARES

Heat the oven to 170°C (325°F/Mark 3).

Grease a rectangular shallow tin, the base measuring 26 × 16 cm (10¼ × 6¼ in), and 3.5 cm (1¼ in) deep. Line base and sides with greaseproof paper; grease the paper.

Cream the margarine and sugar together in a bowl, beating until lightened in colour. In a separate bowl whisk the egg together until frothy. Adding a little at a time, beat about two-thirds of the egg into the creamed mixture, beating well between each addition. Gently stir in the honey, molasses or treacle, ginger and lemon rind, then fold in the flour with the milk and remaining egg to give a soft dropping consistency. Spread half the mixture in the prepared tin. Peel, quarter, core and dice the pears. Sprinkle the fruit evenly over the surface and spread the remaining half of the cake mix over the top. Bake in the centre of the oven for 1 to 1¼ hours or until the cake is firm in the centre and shrinks away slightly from the sides of the tin. Leave to cool in the tin for 10 minutes before lifting from the tin (using the greaseproof paper) and leaving to cool on a wire rack.

Melt the Pear and Apple Spread in a small saucepan over a low heat. Remove the pan from the heat and stir in the lemon juice. Cool until slightly thickened, then spread on top of the cake. Sprinkle with Demerara sugar, and cut into 15 squares to serve.

Wholefood Simnel Cake

I recommend that you wrap this cake in foil and store for three days before putting the almond paste on top and eating. This storage period makes it easier to cut.

Almond Paste
225 g (8 oz) finely ground almonds
225 g (8 oz) light, soft brown sugar
1 egg, beaten
few drops of natural almond essence

Cake
400 g (14 oz) mixed dried fruit
175 g (6 oz) vegetable margarine
175 g (6 oz) dark, soft brown sugar
175 g (6 oz) 100% plain wholewheat flour
3 eggs
50 g (2 oz) sunflower or pumpkin seeds
50 g (2 oz) chopped almonds
2 tablespoons apple juice
2 teaspoons mixed spice
1 teaspoon baking powder
rind of 1 orange or lemon

To finish
1 egg white, lightly beaten

MAKES 10-12 SLICES

Heat the oven to 170°C (325°F/Mark 3).

Grease and line the base and sides of a deep, 18- to 19-cm (7- to 7½-in) round cake tin with a double thickness of greaseproof paper; grease the paper.

First prepare the almond paste. Combine the almonds and sugar together in a bowl and mix thoroughly. In a small basin combine the beaten egg and almond essence. Mix enough of this into the dry ingredients to form a stiff but malleable dough and knead lightly into a ball. Cover and set aside.

Put all the ingredients for the cake into a large bowl and mix well until thoroughly combined. Spoon half the cake mixture into the prepared tin and level the mixture with the back of a spoon. Roll out half the almond paste to a round just slightly smaller than the diameter of the cake tin and lay it on top of the cake mixture in the tin. Spoon the remaining mix on top and bake in the centre of the oven for 2 hours. At this stage check how baking is progressing, lay a sheet of foil over the top of the tin and reduce the oven temperature to 150°C (300°F/Mark 2). Bake for a further 30 to 50 minutes, depending on the size of the tin used, until a skewer inserted in the cake comes out clean. Cool before removing from the tin.

Roll out the remaining almond paste, using the cake tin as a guide to cut out the round. Brush the top of the cake with a little egg white, then cover with the round of almond paste and roll lightly to press it securely onto the cake. Use the back of a knife to create a cross-hatch effect on the paste, then crimp the edge between thumb and forefingers. Decorate with ribbons, chicks and eggs as desired.

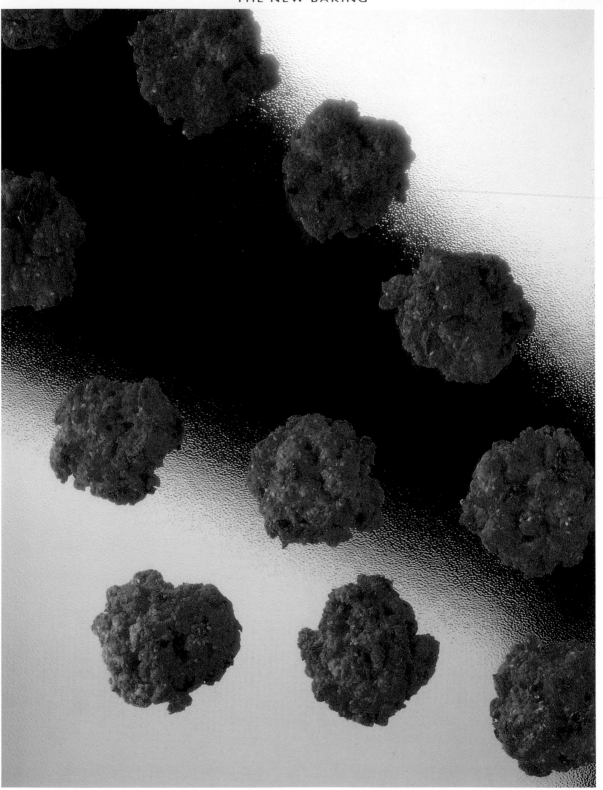

Four-Star Rock Buns

For this recipe use the plump type of apricots and prunes that do not need pre-soaking. The spices, seeds and dried fruits, however, can be changed according to taste or necessity. Experiment!

275 g (10 oz) 85% plain brown flour
25 g (1 oz) wheatgerm
25 g (1 oz) bran
2 teaspoons baking powder
¼ teaspoon grated nutmeg
¼ teaspoon mixed spice
150 g (5 oz) light, soft brown sugar
175 g (6 oz) vegetable margarine
75 g (3 oz) sesame seeds
50 g (2 oz) sunflower seeds
150 g (5 oz) dried apricots
150 g (5 oz) pitted prunes
1 egg, beaten with 2 tablespoons skimmed milk   MAKES 18

Heat the oven to 230°C (450°F/Mark 8).

Grease two baking sheets.

Combine the first seven ingredients in a large bowl. Rub in the margarine until the mixture resembles breadcrumbs. Stir in the seeds and snip the apricots and prunes into the bowl using kitchen scissors. Stir in the beaten egg and milk to form a stiff dough.

Using two forks, pile the mixture into craggy heaps on the greased baking sheets. Bake in the centre of the oven for 12 to 15 minutes until beginning to brown. Use a palette knife to remove the buns to a wire rack to cool. Eat fresh.

Sandwich Cakes

These seem to be the mainstay of British cake-making, so below I have given quite a few ideas and alternatives. All are straightforward and unfussy and I hope that some of my discoveries will inspire you.

But first, it must be said that wholemeal sandwich cakes will never turn out like the towering sponges seen in advertisements for margarines and white flours. For all that, an acceptable, everyday type of sandwich cake can be quickly made, and there is the comfort of knowing exactly what has gone into it!

One-Stage Sandwich Cake

The quickest way to make a sandwich cake. Made with brown flour it gives a 'well-behaved' cake with a slightly rounded top and a fairly close texture.

110 g (4 oz) vegetable margarine	*1 teaspoon baking powder*
110 g (4 oz) light, soft brown sugar	*1 tablespoon tap-hot water*
110 g (4 oz) 85% self-raising brown flour	
2 size 2 eggs	
2 tablespoons wheatgerm	SERVES 6

Heat the oven to 180°C (350°F/Mark 4).

Brush two 18-cm (7-in) sandwich tins with melted margarine. Line the base of each tin with a circle of greaseproof paper; grease the papers.

Put all the ingredients into a bowl and beat well for about 2 minutes or until thoroughly blended and smooth. (Or blend in a food processor.) Divide the mixture equally between the two prepared tins and level the surfaces with the back of a spoon. Bake in the centre of the oven for 25 to 30 minutes. When baked the cakes should feel firm in the centre and should have shrunk away slightly from the sides of the tins. Leave the tins on a wire rack for a minute or so before turning out the cakes. Strip off the base papers. Now put another wire rack on top and holding the two together invert the cakes onto the second rack to sit right side up. Leave to cool. For fillings, see suggestions below.

Flavourings, Fillings and Toppings

Flavourings

These are added to the mixture before baking: the finely grated rind of 1 lemon or orange; spices such as coriander seeds (1 teaspoon, crushed), cardamom (8 seeds, crushed), caraway seeds (1 teaspoon, slightly crushed) may be added in conjunction with citrus rinds or on their own as well as the more usual spices such as cinnamon, mixed spice and ginger; carob powder – blend 1 heaped tablespoon with 2 tablespoons boiling water and leave until cool before adding to the cake mix.

Fillings

I much prefer to use fruit purées rather than jam, but sometimes time does not permit even the making of a swift purée! In this instance I find Pear and Apple Spread a marvellous standby (see page 46). Fruit purées can be speedily made while the cake is baking.

Dried apricot I think this is my favourite. Put 75 g (3 oz) into a small saucepan with enough water to cover. Cook gently, covered, for 10 minutes or until the apricots are soft; process or liquidize to a spreadable purée.

Prunes If the soft, ready-to-eat variety is used, then soaking is unnecessary. Use 150 g (5 oz) prunes and cook as for dried apricots. Add lemon or orange rind and/or juice to sharpen and flavour if liked.

Dates Place 150 g (5 oz) pitted dates in 4 to 6 tablespoons orange juice or water and cook gently, covered, for about 10 minutes or until reduced to a thick purée. This can be flavoured with orange or lemon rind, or mixed spice, or have chopped nuts beaten into it.

Other fruits Apples (using either dried apple rings or the cooking varieties), ripe pears, liquidized with their skins on, bananas mashed with some sherry are good, or crushed seasonal fruits, e.g., nectarines, peaches, soft berries, pitted cherries, etc.

Toppings

On the whole, sandwich cakes made with brown flour tend to have a slightly pockmarked surface, but this is no problem because the cake surfaces can be sprinkled with chopped nuts or seeds. This is a good idea anyway as it avoids the use of any form of sugar for decoration. Try any of the following:

Seeds Sprinkle approximately 2 tablespoons on one or both cakes, e.g., sesame, poppy, chopped pumpkin or sunflower seeds. 1 teaspoon only of caraway seeds. Also try rolled oats, wheatgerm, bran, etc.

Nuts Use as for seeds, e.g., walnuts, almonds, hazelnuts (all finely chopped). (Note: Various nuts are left out here for two reasons; either they are too expensive, or they do not react well to being cooked in this way.)

Traditional Victoria Sandwich

This can be made with either 85% or 100% wholewheat flour, either plain flour plus baking powder, or self-raising flour. You will see I have adopted a slightly different way of making these sponges. The simple device of separating the eggs and folding in the beaten egg whites means the mixture gets just that bit more of a lift so the cakes come out as true Victoria sponges – flat, but with a spongier texture than the One-Stage Sandwich Cake.

110 g (4 oz) vegetable margarine

110 g (4 oz) light, soft brown sugar

2 size 2 eggs, separated

1 tablespoon cold water

110 g (4 oz) 85% self-raising brown flour or

110 g (4 oz) 100% plain wholewheat flour and 1 teaspoon baking powder

SERVES 6

Heat the oven to 180°C (350°F/Mark 4).

Prepare the sandwich tins as for the One-Stage Sandwich Cake above. Put the margarine and sugar in a mixing bowl and beat for 3 or 4 minutes until paler in colour. Separate the eggs, adding the yolks, a little at a time, to the creamed mix and putting the whites in a separate, grease-free bowl. Add the water to the creamed mix and beat thoroughly. Using a large metal spoon, fold in the flour (and the baking powder if used). Whisk the egg whites to a thick foam only – if beaten too stiff the result will be a cobblestone effect on the surface of the cake! Gently fold the egg whites into the cake mixture, then divide it between the two tins and level the surface with the back of a spoon. Bake in the centre of the oven for 25 to 30 minutes. When baked the cakes should feel firm in the centre and show signs of shrinkage from the sides of the tins. Leave the tins on a wire rack for a minute or two, then turn out as in the preceding recipe.

Honey and Lemon Sponge

A slightly more special sponge than the preceding ones, but still quickly made and giving a thicker, more spongy, moist cake with a fresh, light lemon flavour.

175 g (6 oz) dark, soft brown sugar

2 eggs

120 ml (4 fl oz) oil, e.g., sunflower, safflower, groundnut

120 ml (4 fl oz) skimmed milk

2 tablespoons clear honey

175 g (6 oz) plain wholemeal flour

25 g (1 oz) wheatgerm or fine, dry brown breadcrumbs

2 teaspoons baking powder

1 lemon

Filling

110 g (4 oz) fromage frais or skimmed milk cheese

3 tablespoons lemon curd (homemade if possible)

2 teaspoons lemon juice

SERVES 6

Heat the oven to 170°C (325°F/Mark 3).

Brush two 18-cm (7-in) sandwich tins with melted margarine. Line the base of each tin with a circle of greaseproof paper; grease the papers.

Put all the ingredients except the lemon into a bowl. Grate in the lemon rind and add the juice of half the lemon. Beat all the ingredients together until smooth. (It will be an unusually slack mix.) Pour an equal quantity of the mixture into each of the prepared tins and bake in the centre of the oven for about 45 minutes or until the cakes shrink slightly from the sides of the tins. Remove from the oven and run a knife around between cake and tin to loosen the edges. Leave the tins to cool on a wire rack for a minute or two before turning out. Strip off the base papers and leave the right way up until cold.

To make the filling, simply combine the fromage frais and lemon curd in a bowl, adding the remaining lemon juice to taste. Use this mixture to sandwich the cake. I prefer to chill this cake just a little before serving.

One-Stage Brownies

Just put everything into a bowl, stir and bake! The traditional American fudge frosting seems to make it all too rich and sweet. Instead these brownies just have nuts scattered over the top which, to me, is quicker, easier and better all round. If really not sweet enough for your taste, give the baked brownies a dusting of Demerara sugar which has been ground until fine in a liquidizer.

Cake
150 g (5 oz) vegetable margarine
225 g (8 oz) dark, soft brown sugar
3 eggs
1 teaspoon natural vanilla essence
40 g (1½ oz) carob or cocoa powder
110 g (4 oz) 85% plain brown flour
1½ teaspoons baking powder
2 tablespoons bran flakes

Topping
100 g (4 oz) assorted chopped nuts and seeds,
   (e.g., almond, walnut, hazelnut, Brazil,
   sunflower, pumpkin, sesame)

MAKES 18

Heat the oven to 180°C (350°F/Mark 4).

Grease and line a shallow, rectangular tin, 27 × 16.5 × 3 cm (10½ × 6½ × 1¼ in); grease the lining paper.

Put all the ingredients into a bowl and stir until thoroughly blended. Spread evenly in the prepared tin, scatter with the nuts and seeds and bake in the centre of the oven for 50 minutes. When baked the cake will show signs of shrinkage from the sides of the tin and a skewer inserted in the centre will come out clean. Invert onto a large baking sheet, strip off the base paper, place a wire rack over the cake and, holding the cake sandwiched between the baking sheet and wire rack, turn nut side up to sit on the wire rack to cool. Slice into bars using a sharp scalloped knife.

Hot Honey Buns

This seems a strange recipe but the buns turn out beautifully. They are good at teatime as a quick alternative to scones. Maple syrup may be used instead of honey, if you prefer.

Buns
225 g (8 oz) vegetable margarine
200 g (7 oz) light, soft brown sugar
75 g (3 oz) 85% plain brown flour
75 g (3 oz) 100% plain wholewheat flour
6 eggs
1 tablespoon ground cinnamon
25 g (1 oz) wheatgerm

Topping
6 tablespoons clear honey or maple syrup
110 g (4 oz) chopped walnuts   MAKES 16

Heat the oven to 200°C (400°F/Mark 6).

Use a deep, 12-hole bun or muffin tin, each cup of 60-ml (4-tablespoon) capacity. Brush liberally with melted margarine.

In a large bowl combine the margarine, brown sugar and 2 tablespoons of the measured flour. Beat vigorously until lightened in colour. Beat the eggs into the mixture one at a time. It will curdle by the time you have added the third egg, but do not worry, keep going until all the eggs have been added. Stir in the remaining flour, the cinnamon and wheatgerm. Spoon the mixture into each cup, filling them almost to the top (this mixture will make 16 buns which should give some guide as to how much mixture to use). Bake in the centre of the oven for 20 minutes.

Meanwhile, combine the honey or maple syrup and the chopped walnuts in a bowl. When the 20 minutes are up, spoon a little of the mixture over each bun, keeping back enough for the second batch of four to be baked. Bake for a further 5 minutes. Free the buns by sliding a knife round the edge. Transfer to a wire rack, but only for a minute or two, they are delicious hot. Bake the remaining batch in the same way.

Spiced Prune and Apple Cake

This cake looks better ready-sliced. It has a better fresh fruit flavour than many rich fruit cakes.

175 g (6 oz) ready-to-eat prunes, pitted and
  chopped
110 g (4 oz) chopped walnuts
1 medium-sized cooking apple, chopped
175 g (6 oz) dark, soft brown sugar
170 ml (6 fl oz) vegetable oil
2 eggs
½ teaspoon natural vanilla essence
175 g (6 oz) 85% plain brown flour
1½ teaspoons baking powder
¼ teaspoon ground cloves
½ teaspoon ground cinnamon
½ teaspoon ground ginger
¼ teaspoon freshly grated nutmeg   MAKES 10-12 SLICES

Heat the oven to 170°C (325°F/Mark 3).

Grease a sloping-sided, deep, rectangular tin, the base measuring 20 × 16 cm (8 × 4 in) and 7 cm (2¾ in) deep. Line the base with greaseproof paper; grease the paper and dust the sides of the tin with flour.

Combine the chopped prunes, walnuts and apple together in a bowl and toss well to mix.

In a separate mixing bowl combine the sugar, oil and eggs. Beat together until light and opaque. Stir in the dry ingredients followed by all but about 2 tablespoons of the chopped fruit and nut mixture. Transfer the mixture to the prepared tin and level the top with the back of a spoon. Sprinkle the reserved fruit and nut mixture over the surface and bake in the centre of the oven for 1¾ to 2 hours, or until a thin metal skewer, inserted into the centre of the cake, comes out clean. Cool in the tin before turning out onto a wire rack. Serve the cake sliced and arranged on a plate.

PASTRIES

Table of Quantities for
Basic (and Cheese) Wholewheat Shortcrust Pastry

100% plain wholewheat flour	Vegetable margarine	Baking powder	Water	Cheese Pastry*
100 g (4 oz)	40 g (1½ oz)	1 teaspoon	2 tablespoons	50 g (2 oz)
150 g (5 oz)	50 g (2 oz)	1½ teaspoons	2½ tablespoons	75 g (3 oz)
175 g (6 oz)	60 g (2½ oz)	1¾ teaspoons	2-3 tablespoons	110 g (4 oz)
200 g (7 oz)	75 g (3 oz)	2 teaspoons	3 tablespoons	110 to 150 g (4 to 5 oz)
225 g (8 oz)	85 g (3½ oz)	2¼ teaspoons	3-4 tablespoons	150 g (5 oz)

(Before starting, please read Baking Methods – Pastry, page 16.)

* Use grated Cheddar or Edam.

Individual Curd Cheese Cakes

Basic Wholewheat Shortcrust Pastry

Put the flour, margarine and baking powder in a large bowl. The margarine can be rubbed into the dry ingredients either by using the fingertips, or a fork, or using a criss-cross cutting action with two knives. When the mixture resembles breadcrumbs, mix in the grated cheese, if used, then add all the water at once and stir with a spatula until the mixture begins to hold together. Then finish by gently pressing the dough into one large ball using your hands.

Turn out onto a lightly floured surface, knead briefly and lightly, then roll out to 3mm (⅛ in) thick and use as required.

Other suggested additions:
Ranging from 1 to 2 teaspoons (depending on the quantity of pastry used), any one of the following flavourings can be used: mustard powder, curry powder, herbs (dried or fresh), grated orange and lemon rind.

To give pastry extra crunch, roll it out using fine cornmeal instead of flour – a little trickier to manage, but worth the effort.

Quick Wholewheat Flaky Pastry

Delia Smith first introduced me to this technique and it is with her permission that I give the recipe here, with one main alteration: the plain white flour of the original recipe is replaced with 100% plain wholewheat. The result is very satisfactory. Only one hiccup: remember to freeze the margarine for about 1 hour before using. I have used this specific brand of margarine because it is suitably hard and is made entirely of vegetables oils.

225 g (8 oz) 100% plain wholewheat flour
175 g (6 oz) Tomor kosher margarine, frozen
    hard
6-7 tablespoons cold water, to mix.

Put the flour in a mixing bowl. Holding a wrapped end of the block of margarine, dip it into the flour, then coarsely grate it into the bowl. Dip the fat frequently into the flour and stop often to toss the grated shreds in the flour with a fork. Spoon in 6 tablespoons water, stir and start to bring the dough together using first a spatula, then your hands. Use the additional water if necessary. Bring the dough up to form a ball, then wrap in cling film and chill for 30 minutes before using as required.

Ratatouille and Prawn Gougère

I have given two alternatives for the type of flour used in the choux paste. Whilst the combination of wholewheat and strong flour makes a marginally better choux paste (slightly crisper with a better rise), sometimes you just do not happen to have the two types of flour when you want them, so I have given an all-wholewheat choux paste as a very acceptable alternative.

Wholewheat choux paste

either *50 g (2 oz) 100% plain wholewheat flour and 75 g (3 oz) strong white unbleached flour*
or *150 g (5 oz) 100% plain wholewheat flour*
110 g (4 oz) vegetable margarine
275 ml (½ pint) water
3 eggs
½ teaspoon mixed herbs
salt and freshly ground black pepper
50 g (2 oz) grated cheese

Filling

2 tablespoons vegetable oil
1 medium-sized onion, coarsely chopped
1 large clove garlic, crushed
1 225-g (8-oz) aubergine, cubed
3 small courgettes, halved lengthwise then cut across in 1-cm (½-in) thick slices
1 pepper, de-seeded and coarsely chopped
1 teaspoon dried basil
1 395-g (14-oz) can tomatoes
1 teaspoon tomato purée
110 g (4 oz) peeled prawns

SERVES 4

You will need a dish, preferably enamelware or stainless steel, with a capacity of 1 litre 700 mls (3 pints) capacity and about 4.5 cm (1¾ in) deep. Grease lightly.

Start by making the choux paste. Put the margarine and water in a medium-sized saucepan and bring to the boil. As soon as the water boils and all the margarine has melted shoot in all the flour in one go and stir vigorously. Within about a minute the mixture will form a smooth ball around the spoon. Remove the pan from the heat. Beat for a further 30 seconds, then break in the eggs, one at a time, beating well between each addition. Beat in the herbs and a little seasoning. Cover and leave aside.

Heat the oven to 200°C (400°F/Mark 6).

Prepare the filling. In a large saucepan heat the oil and stir in the onion and garlic. Cover and cook gently for 5 minutes. Uncover, add the aubergine, courgettes and pepper. Sprinkle in the basil, stir, re-cover and cook gently for a further 5 minutes before adding the tomatoes. Cover and cook for 5 minutes, then uncover and cook until the vegetables are almost cooked and the liquid has evaporated to give a good sauce consistency. Stir in the tomato purée and prawns and remove from the heat. Taste and add a little seasoning if necessary.

Spoon the choux paste in an even band around the edge of the tin, then the vegetable and prawn filling in the centre. Sprinkle the choux with cheese and put in the upper third of the oven to bake for about 50 minutes. Check to make sure the choux paste has cooked through before serving.

Eccles-Style Pastries

Eccles cakes have always been a favourite of mine. So too have the type of poppy seed fillings found in some rich continental breads. Here I have tried to combine the two – a poppy seed mixture for an Eccles-style pastry. I think the result is good, without being quite so high in fat and sugar as the traditional variety.

Pastry
225 g (8 oz) Quick Wholewheat Flaky Pastry
(page 59) using 225 g (8 oz) 100% plain
wholewheat flour

SERVES 25

Filling
75 g (3 oz) poppy seeds
50 g (2 oz) Demerara sugar plus extra for
sprinkling
75 g (3 oz) chopped walnuts
1 cooking apple, finely chopped
grated rind of 1 lemon

Have the Quick Wholewheat Flaky Pastry chilling in the fridge whilst the filling is being prepared.

Put the poppy seeds into a bowl and cover with plenty of boiling water. Leave aside for an hour, then drain thoroughly and transfer to a liquidizer or food processor. Blend for 2 minutes, add the sugar and blend for a further minute. Return the poppy seeds to the bowl and stir in the remaining ingredients.

Heat the oven to 220°C (425°F/Mark 7).

On a lightly floured surface roll out the pastry to a large round about 3 mm (⅛ in) thick. Cut out rounds using a plain 9.5-cm (3¾-in) cutter. Gather up the pastry trimmings, wrap and refrigerate until ready to re-roll them. Put a teaspoon of poppy seed mixture in the centre of each round. Dampen half the pastry edge of each round, then bring the edges up to the centre and pinch together well. Turn over so the pinched edges are underneath and roll lightly to flatten to about ½ cm (¼ in) thick. Transfer to well greased baking sheets. With a sharp knife score each pastry across 3 or 4 times, dampen with water and sprinkle with Demerara sugar. Re-roll any pastry trimmings and repeat the procedure. Bake in the centre of the oven for 15 to 20 minutes or until lightly browned. Cool on a wire rack. Best eaten fresh.

Tomato and Pesto Tart

I have adopted this method of making a tomato tart because it seems the best way of retaining the fresh flavour. If the tart can be cooked on a good, solid baking sheet it will help to prevent the pastry base becoming soggy. Pesto – Italian basil sauce – is now available in delicatessens and some supermarkets.

Cheese and oatmeal pastry
150 g (5 oz) 85% plain brown flour
50 g (2 oz) fine oatmeal
75 g (3 oz) vegetable margarine
50 g (2 oz) grated Cheddar cheese
25 g (1 oz) grated Parmesan cheese
salt and freshly ground black pepper
2-3 tablespoons water

Filling
6 medium-sized tomatoes (approximately
   560 g/1¼ lbs)
2 eggs
150 ml (¼ pint) single cream or creamed
   smetana
2 tablespoons pesto
salt and freshly ground black pepper
3 tablespoons finely chopped parsley
3 tablespoons finely chopped spring onions

Topping
2 tablespoons grated Cheddar cheese
2 tablespoons grated Parmesan cheese

MAKES 8-10 SLICES

Heat the oven to 200°C (400°F/Mark 6) and place a heavy baking sheet in it to heat. You will need a tart tin measuring 24 to 27 cm (9½ to 10½ in) in diameter.

To make the pastry, place the flour and oatmeal in a bowl and rub in the margarine to give a uniform fine crumb. Sprinkle in the cheeses and add a little salt and plenty of freshly ground black pepper. Toss together lightly with a fork. Add the water and mix to form a dough that leaves the side of the bowl clean. Roll out and use to line the tart tin. Prick the base thoroughly with a fork, transfer the tin to the baking sheet and bake in the centre of the oven for 15 minutes. Check that the pastry base is cooked through. If not, continue baking for a further 5 minutes. Break the eggs for the filling into a bowl, whisk, and use a little to paint over the pastry case. Return to the oven again to bake for a further 5 minutes, then remove.

Whisk the cream and pesto into the beaten eggs and season to taste. Peel and slice the tomatoes. Strew about half the chopped parsley and spring onions on the base of the baked pastry case. Arrange the tomato slices in overlapping concentric circles on top and sprinkle over the remaining onion and parsley mixture. With the tin still on the baking sheet return it to the centre of the oven before spooning the egg mixture in. Bake for 20 minutes, sprinkle with the combined Cheddar and Parmesan cheeses, then bake for a further 10 minutes. Pre-heat the grill to hot and grill the tart briefly to brown the cheeses. Serve warm.

Wholewheat Almond Tarts

Nutty, buttery, almondy and delicious! You might wonder about boiling the filling with two beaten eggs in it but don't worry – it does work!

Filling
175 g (6 oz) dark, soft brown sugar
150 g (5 oz) currants
75 g (3 oz) chopped, unblanched almonds
75 g (3 oz) vegetable margarine
2 eggs, beaten
4 tablespoons single cream
1 teaspoon natural almond essence

Pastry
110 g (4 oz) 85% self-raising brown flour
110 g (4 oz) 100% plain, wholewheat flour
110 g (4 oz) vegetable margarine
1-2 tablespoons water

MAKES 16

Heat the oven to 190°C (375°F/Mark 5).

Grease a 12-hole bun tin.

To make the filling put all the ingredients together in a saucepan and bring to the boil, stirring. Boil for 2 minutes, stirring continuously then remove from the heat and leave to cool.

Prepare the pastry by combining the flours and margarine in a bowl. Cut in the margarine until the mixture has a rather lumpy, uneven texture. Sprinkle in 1 tablespoon of water and press the mix together to form a dough. This quantity makes 16 tarts, so this will probably mean baking in two batches. Roll out the pastry to 3 mm (⅛ in) thick and use a 8.5-cm (3¼-in) fluted cutter to line the tin. Re-roll pastry scraps to enable you to cut out 16 rounds.

Spoon the cooled filling into the pastry tart shells and bake in the centre of the oven for 20 minutes. Cool on a wire rack before serving.

Wholewheat Lemon and Almond Tart

A good family pudding. Grind the almonds in their skins in a processor, liquidizer or nutmill.

Pastry
75 g (3 oz) 100% plain wholewheat flour
25 g (1 oz) 85% plain brown flour
¼ teaspoon baking powder
50 g (2 oz) vegetable margarine, chilled
about 3 tablespoons water

SERVES 8

Filling
50 g (2 oz) unskinned almonds, ground
3 tablespoons home-made lemon curd or Seville
*   orange marmalade*
75 g (3 oz) vegetable margarine
75 g (3 oz) light, soft brown sugar
1 size 2 egg, lightly beaten
110 g (4 oz) 100% plain wholewheat flour
1 teaspoon baking powder
rind and juice of 1 lemon
1-2 tablespoons milk
25 g (1 oz) skinned, halved almonds

Heat the oven to 200°C (400°F/Mark 6). Place a good, solid baking sheet in the oven to heat. You will also need a 20- to 21.5-cm (8- to 8½-in) diameter enamel pie plate.

Rub the margarine into the flours and baking powder until the mixture resembles breadcrumbs. Add just sufficient water to mix to a firm dough that leaves the side of the bowl clean. Roll out to a round slightly larger than that of the pie plate; line this, trimming away the excess pastry and crimping the edge attractively between thumb and forefinger. Scatter the surface with half the ground almonds, then spoon over the lemon curd or marmalade. Spread out carefully to avoid disturbing the ground almonds. (If you use marmalade this process may be a bit easier if you warm it first.)

To make the filling beat the margarine and sugar together until a little paler in colour. Add the beaten egg in three batches, beating well between each addition. Fold in the remaining ground almonds, flour and baking powder with the grated lemon rind and juice. Mix to a soft, dropping consistency with a little milk if necessary. Spoon the mixture over the lemon curd and spread it gently and evenly with a palette knife up to the crimped pastry edge. Scatter the surface with the halved almonds, then transfer to the oven to bake on the baking sheet for 15 minutes. Reduce the oven temperature to 150°C (300°F/Mark 2) for a further 30 to 40 minutes. Serve warm or cold with a sharp fruit sauce.

Rum and Buttermilk Pie

175 g (6 oz) Basic Wholewheat Shortcrust
  Pastry (see page 58) using 175 g (6 oz) 100%
  plain wholewheat flour
4 eggs
2 tablespoons 100% wholewheat or 85% plain
  brown flour
425 ml (¾ pint) buttermilk

about 50 g (2 oz) sugar
75 g (3 oz) vegetable margarine, melted
1 teaspoon natural vanilla essence
3 tablespoons rum

SERVES 12

Heat the oven to 220°C (425°F/Mark 7).

Put a good solid baking sheet to heat in the centre of the oven. You will also need a round, sloping-sided pie tin measuring 4 cm (1½ in) deep, base 18 cm (7 in), top 24 cm (9½ in).

Roll out the pastry and use to line the pie tin. Trim the excess pastry from the rim and crimp the pastry edge attractively between thumb and forefinger.

Break the eggs into a bowl and add the flour. Whisk together until thoroughly combined and smooth. Add the remaining ingredients and whisk again until thoroughly mixed. (If you have a liquidizer, put all the ingredients in together and blend until smooth.) Taste for sweetness and add a little more sugar if necessary. Pour into the prepared pastry case and transfer (carefully) to bake on the baking sheet for 10 minutes. Lower the heat to 180°C (350°F/Mark 4) and continue to bake for a further 20 to 25 minutes or until the filling is set. Serve warm with a thin, pouring, apricot sauce.

Honeyed Custard Tart

175 g (6 oz) Basic Wholewheat Shortcrust
  Pastry (see page 58) using 175 g (6 oz) 100%
  plain wholewheat flour

Filling
3 eggs
275 ml (½ pint) milk
2 tablespoons honey
freshly grated nutmeg   SERVES 6

Heat the oven to 190°C (375°F/Mark 5) and put a thick baking sheet in it to heat. You will also need a round, sloping-sided pie tin, 4 cm (1½ in) deep, base 18 cm (7 in), top 24 cm (9½ in). Roll out the pastry and use to line the pie tin. Trim the excess pastry from the rim and crimp the pastry edge attractively between thumb and forefinger. Prick the base well with a fork and bake on the baking sheet for 15 minutes.

   Meanwhile separate one of the eggs putting the egg white into a bowl and reserving the egg yolk. Whisk the egg white a little with a fork. When the pastry case has had the initial baking time remove it from the oven and brush with egg white. Leave aside whilst you add the reserved yolk to the remaining egg white. Add the other two eggs, the milk and honey and whisk until thoroughly mixed. Return the pie tin to the baking sheet. Spoon the filling into the pastry case and grate a generous amount of nutmeg over the top. Reduce the oven temperature to 180°C (350°F/Mark 4) and bake the tart for about 40 minutes or until the custard has set. A knife inserted in the centre should come out clean. Serve warm or cold.

Broccoli, Prawn and Feta Cheese Quiche

110 g (4 oz) Cheese Wholewheat Pastry (see page 58) using 110 g (4 oz) 100% plain wholewheat flour

Filling
110 g (4 oz) broccoli florets, no bigger than a thumbnail
110 g (4 oz) peeled prawns
50 g (2 oz) Feta cheese
150 ml (¼ pint) soured cream
275 ml (½ pint) skimmed milk
3 eggs
salt and freshly ground black pepper
freshly grated nutmeg or a little mace

MAKES 8 SLICES

Heat the oven to 200°C (400°F/Mark 6) and put a baking sheet in it to heat. You will also need a round, sloping-sided pie tin 4 cm (1½ in) deep, base 18 cm (7 in), top 24 cm (9½ in).

Roll out the pastry and use to line the pie tin. Trim any excess away from the rim of the tin, then crimp the edge attractively between thumb and forefinger. Prick the base and side well with a fork and bake on a baking sheet in the centre of the oven for 15 to 20 minutes, then remove and reduce the oven temperature to 180°C (350°F/Mark 4).

Meanwhile put the broccoli in a small saucepan, pour over just sufficient boiling water to cover it and add a little salt. Bring to the boil, cook for 2 minutes, then drain in a colander or sieve. Cool under running cold water, drain well, then pat dry on absorbent kitchen paper. Place the florets in the pastry case. Pat the prawns dry and add to the broccoli. Lastly, crumble in the Feta cheese. In a bowl whisk together the remaining ingredients adding a little salt and some freshly ground black pepper to taste. Put the quiche back in the oven on the baking sheet before spooning in the egg mixture. Sprinkle with grated nutmeg or mace. Bake for about 50 minutes or until the filling is set and lightly puffed. Serve warm.

Sweetcorn and Peanut Pie

This sounds a bit odd, but it works rather well. The combination of flavours is good, the surprising element being that the peanuts take on a texture rather like that of water chestnuts.

110 g (4 oz) Cheese Wholewheat Pastry (see
   page 58) using 110 g (4 oz) 100% plain
   wholewheat flour

Filling
2 tablespoons vegetable oil
½ pepper, de-seeded and diced
110 g (4 oz) mushrooms, thinly sliced
50 g (2 oz) salted peanuts, chopped
200 g (7 oz) sweetcorn kernels
½ teaspoon dried basil, or 1 teaspoon fresh
   basil, chopped
275 ml (½ pint) skimmed milk
150 ml (¼ pint) soured cream
3 eggs
1 tablespoon tomato purée
salt and freshly ground black pepper

MAKES 8 SLICES

Heat the oven to 190°C (375°F/Mark 5) and place a baking sheet in it to heat. You will need a round, sloping-sided pie tin 4 cm (1½ in) deep, base 18 cm (7 in), top 24 cm (9½ in).

Roll out the pastry and use to line the pie tin. Trim the excess pastry from the rim, then crimp the pastry edge attractively between thumb and forefinger. Prick the base and side well with a fork and bake on the baking sheet in the centre of the oven for 20 minutes. Remove and reduce the oven temperature to 180°C (350°F/Mark 4).

Meanwhile start to prepare the filling. Heat the oil in a frying pan. Add the diced pepper to the pan and fry gently for 5 minutes before stirring in the sliced mushrooms. Continue cooking gently for a further 5 minutes, then add the chopped peanuts, sweetcorn and basil. Stir to mix thoroughly, then remove the pan from the heat.

In a bowl whisk together the remaining ingredients. Season with a little salt and freshly ground black pepper to taste.

Sprinkle the vegetable and peanut mixture into the pastry case, then replace it on the baking sheet in the oven. Carefully pour the egg mixture into the pastry case, then bake for about 50 minutes or until the filling is set and slightly puffed. Serve warm or cold.

Russian-Style Cabbage Pie

It tastes good and it is cheap! This is a pie that needs no dish!

Pastry
225 g (8 oz) Quick Wholewheat Flaky Pastry
  (see page 59)
beaten egg, to glaze

Filling
2 tablespoons vegetable oil
1 onion, chopped
1 teacup cracked wheat (bulgar/burghul)
2½ teacups hot vegetable stock
450 g (1 lb) Savoy cabbage, finely sliced
¾ teaspoon dill weed
2 teaspoons tamari or light soy sauce
2 teaspoons lemon juice
freshly ground black pepper
4 hard-boiled eggs

MAKES 10-12 SLICES

Heat the oven to 220°C (425°F/Mark 7).

Have ready a large, greased baking sheet.

The pastry can remain chilling in the fridge whilst the filling is made and cooled.

In a large saucepan, heat the oil and fry the onion until golden. Stir in the cracked wheat and cook for half a minute before pouring in the hot stock. Cover and cook gently for 5 minutes. Whilst this is cooking, put the finely sliced cabbage into a large heatproof colander. Pour a kettleful of boiling water over the cabbage and then, when cool enough, squeeze out the excess moisture and stir the cabbage into the contents of the saucepan. Add the dill weed, tamari and lemon juice and a little freshly ground black pepper. Cover and continue to cook gently for a further 10 minutes. At this stage taste and adjust the seasoning if necessary, then cover, remove from the heat and leave until cold.

Roll out a third of the pastry to a round, about 25.5 cm (10 in) in diameter. Transfer this to the baking sheet. Spread a layer of the filling on the pastry leaving a clear border about 1 cm (½ in) wide. Place a hard-boiled egg in each quarter on top of the filling and cover with the remaining mixture. It will be heaped up quite considerably. Roll out the remaining pastry to a larger round about 35 cm (14 in) in diameter. Brush the pastry border with beaten egg and lay the larger round over the filling. Ease the pastry into place, pressing the edge lightly with the side of your hand, to seal. Trim off the excess, then knock up the pastry edge with the back of a knife and scallop it with the knife and forefinger. Re-roll any pastry trimmings and cut out leaves to decorate the top of the pie. Make a steam hole in the centre and brush all over with beaten egg. Bake in the centre of the oven for 15 minutes, then reduce the oven temperature to 190°C (375°F/Mark 5) for a further 15 minutes or until the pastry is browned and crisp. Serve warmed with creamed smetana.

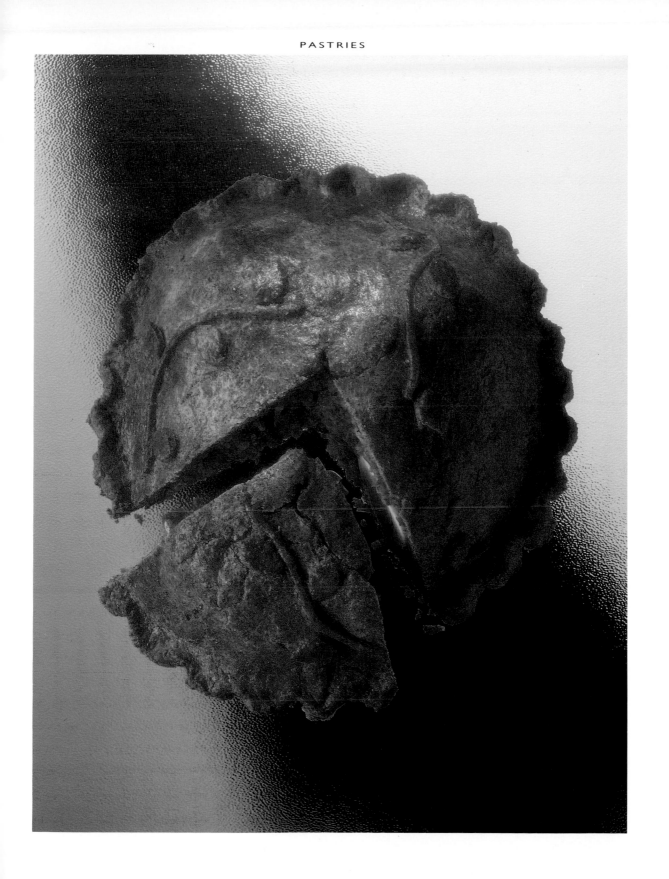

Hot and Spiced Pea and Potato Pasties

If you are unused to dealing with fresh chillies, a word of warning: try to avoid getting the juices anywhere near your eyes or mouth or under your fingernails.

Pastry

225 g (8 oz) Basic Wholewheat Shortcrust
  Pastry (see page 58) using 225 g (8 oz) 100%
  plain wholewheat flour

MAKES 7

Filling

2 tablespoons vegetable oil
1 onion, finely chopped
1 fresh chilli
2 teaspoons peeled and finely chopped fresh
  ginger
225 g (8 oz) boiled potatoes, diced
150 g (5 oz) green peas
¼ teaspoon garam masala
1 teaspoon crushed coriander seeds
2 teaspoons lemon juice
salt to taste
beaten egg, to glaze

First prepare the filling, then this can cool whilst you make the pastry. Heat the oil in a medium-sized saucepan and gently fry the chopped onion until golden and softened. Halve the chilli lengthways and hold under cold running water to flush out the seeds. Chop finely and add to the onion with the ginger and 4 tablespoons of water. Cover and cook gently for 5 minutes before adding the remaining ingredients. Cover again and heat gently for a further 5 minutes, then leave to cool.

Heat the oven to 220°C (425°F/Mark 7).

Roll out the pastry to a large round about 3 mm (⅛ in) thick. Use a saucer as a guide to cut out rounds about 15 cm (6 in) in diameter. Put about one-seventh of the filling on half the circle of pastry. Dampen the pastry edge of the half circle, fold the other half of the pastry over to enclose the filling and press the edges together to seal. To ensure a good seal and to decorate, press the pastry edge with the tines of a fork. Place on a lightly greased baking sheet and brush with beaten egg. Bake in the top third of the oven for about 20 minutes or until nicely browned. Serve hot or cold; good with yogurt.

Courgette and Wensleydale Pasties

For the filling you can fry the almonds in the oil and remove before adding the onion, but it is very easy to over-brown them. The alternative is to brown them in the heating oven which takes longer but is a little safer.

Pastry
225 g (8 oz) Quick Wholewheat Flaky Pastry
  (see page 59)

Filling
2 tablespoons vegetable oil
50 g (2 oz) browned almonds, slivered
1 onion, chopped
375 g (14 oz) courgettes
½ teaspoon dill weed
2 teaspoons lemon juice
75 g (3 oz) crumbled Wensleydale cheese
salt and freshly ground black pepper
beaten egg, to glaze
sesame seeds, to finish

MAKES 10

Have the flaky pastry wrapped and chilling in the fridge whilst you prepare the filling.

Heat the oil in a medium-sized saucepan and fry the onion gently for 5 minutes, covered. Meanwhile top and tail the courgettes, then quarter them lengthways. Cut the courgette across into 1-cm (½-in) thick slices. Add to the onion with the dill weed, then cover and continue to cook gently for a further 15 minutes or until just tender. Remove from the heat and cool a little before stirring in the almonds and cheese. Taste and season if necessary, then leave until cold. Whilst the filling is cooling heat the oven to 220°C (425°F/Mark 7).

Roll out the pastry to a large round and follow the instructions for making Hot and Spiced Pea and Potato Pasties on page 72.

Put the pasties on a baking sheet, brush with beaten egg and sprinkle with sesame seeds before baking in the top third of the oven for about 25 minutes. These pasties are better served cold.

Mushroom Pâté in Herbed Yeast Pastry

Perhaps a daunting list of ingredients, but very easily dealt with! Serve this loaf sliced cold with salad and a yogurt dressing.

Pâté

450 g (1 lb) mushrooms, chopped
2 stalks celery, chopped
2 small onions, chopped
2 tablespoons vegetable oil
¼ teaspoon rosemary
¼ teaspoon dried thyme
2 eggs, beaten
150 g (5 oz) ricotta or curd cheese
110 g (4 oz) chopped walnuts
75 g (3 oz) wholewheat breadcrumbs
75 g (3 oz) coarsely chopped watercress leaves
salt and freshly ground black pepper
4 tablespoons Madeira
2 teaspoons mushroom ketchup (optional)
1-2 teaspoons lemon juice

Yeast pastry

225 g (8 oz) 100% plain wholewheat flour
½ teaspoon salt
½ teaspoon mixed, dried herbs
150 ml (¼ pint) tepid water
15 g (½ oz) fresh yeast
25-mg Vitamin C tablet
1 teaspoon vegetable oil

Glaze

Milk or water or beaten egg
A few sesame seeds

MAKES 12-16 SLICES

You will need a rectangular loaf tin, base measurement 20 × 10 cm (8 × 4 in) by 7 cm (2¾ in) high; grease liberally.

Heat the oil in a large frying pan. Add the mushrooms, celery and onions. Sprinkle in the herbs, then stir and heat for about 8 minutes or until all the excess liquid has evaporated. Put the pan aside from the heat and leave to cool. Add the beaten eggs, crumbled ricotta cheese and continue to add the remaining ingredients one by one in the order given above. Use a food processor or liquidizer to blend the mixture *briefly*. (You will have to do this in several batches.) Try not to blend it until smooth but keep some texture in the mixture. Taste and season further if necessary.

To make the pastry, have the flour, salt and herbs ready in a bowl. Measure the water and whisk in the yeast and Vitamin C tablet. When these are dissolved, add the oil, then shoot the liquid straight into the dry ingredients. Stir until the mixture comes together to form a dough, then turn out onto a clean work surface and knead for 5 minutes. Cover with the upturned bowl and leave to rest for 10 minutes.

Put aside one-third of the dough and roll out the rest to a rectangle about 25.5 × 38 cm (10 × 15 in). Ease this into the tin. The dough will accommodate itself quite comfortably without too many folds and pleats. Spoon in the pâté mix and roll out the remaining third of dough to a surface area slightly bigger than the top of the tin. Brush the pastry edges slightly overhanging the rim of the tin with milk, water or beaten egg. Lay the top piece in position and press the edges together. Use a pair of scissors to cut the dough to a neat edge that stands rather higher than the rim of the tin. Pinch this with thumb and forefinger to give an attractive, well-sealed edge. Make steam-holes in the top of the pie and re-roll any pastry trimmings to decorate with leaves or tassles if you wish, but a word of caution – don't go overboard with the decorations. With yeast pastry this can make the top far too thick. It is then hard to cut and not pleasant to eat. Brush the top of the pie and sprinkle with sesame seeds. Enclose in a plastic bag and leave in a warm place to rise for 15 to 20 minutes.

Heat the oven to 200°C (400°F/Mark 6).

Bake in the centre of the oven for 30 minutes. At this stage cover the top of the loaf with a sheet of foil and reduce the oven temperature to 180°C (350°F/Mark 4). Bake for a further 1 hour. Remove from the oven and leave to become cold before slicing and serving.

Chestnut and Bacon Tart

Remembering to soak the chestnuts overnight is, to my mind, easier than peeling them fresh; but it is up to you! You will need 110 g (4 oz) fresh chestnuts.

Pastry
75 g (3 oz) 100% plain wholewheat flour
75 g (3 oz) 85% plain brown flour
50 g (2 oz) vegetable margarine
½ teaspoon baking powder

MAKES 8-10 SLICES

Filling
50 g (2 oz) dried chestnuts, soaked overnight
5 rashers unsmoked back bacon
1 medium-sized onion, diced
275 ml (½ pint) half-cream (12% butterfat)
2 size 2 eggs
1 tablespoon strong French mustard
salt and freshly ground black pepper
freshly grated nutmeg

Heat the oven to 190°C (375°F/Mark 5).

Put a good, solid baking sheet in the oven to heat at the same time. You will also need a fluted or plain tart tin, base measurement 23 to 24 cm (9 to 9½ in). Put the chestnuts in a pan with boiling water to cover and boil gently for about 20 minutes until softened. Then drain, cool and crumble.

Make the pastry in the usual way by rubbing the margarine into the dry ingredients. Add just sufficient water to mix to a stiff unsticky dough. Roll out on a floured working surface and use to line the tart tin. Prick the base well with a fork and bake on the baking sheet in the oven for 15 to 20 minutes.

Remove the rinds from the bacon and cut into small strips. Put to heat in a frying pan and fry until the fat runs and the bacon is just crispy. Using a slotted spoon, remove the bacon from the pan and drain on absorbent kitchen paper. Cook the onion in the fat remaining in the pan. When softened and golden, add to the bacon.

In a bowl whisk together the cream, eggs and mustard and season to taste with salt and freshly ground black pepper.

Remove the tart shell from the oven on the baking sheet. Sprinkle the chestnuts, bacon and onion into the base of the tart. Return the tart tin, still on the baking sheet, to the oven shelf *before* pouring in the cream mixture. Grate a little more nutmeg over the surface and leave to bake at 180°C (350°F/Mark 4) for about 50 minutes. The surface will gently puff up when baked. Serve warm.

Green Lentil and Split-Pea Plait

Pastry

either *175 g (6 oz) Basic Wholewheat*
    Shortcrust Pastry (page 58) using 175 g
    (6 oz) 100% plain wholewheat flour
or *Quick Wholewheat Flaky Pastry (see*
    method on page 59) made with
175 g (6 oz) 100% plain wholewheat flour
125 g (6 oz) Tomor kosher margarine, frozen
    hard
5-6 tablespoons cold water

SERVES 6-8

Filling

570 ml (1 pint) vegetable stock
110 g (4 oz) green or yellow split peas
175 g (6 oz) green lentils
2-3 tablespoons vegetable oil
1 onion, chopped
2 carrots, chopped
2 stalks celery, chopped
1 pepper, de-seeded and chopped
½ teaspoon dried marjoram
¼ teaspoon dried thyme
1 clove garlic, crushed
2 tablespoons chopped parsley or watercress
1 egg, beaten
salt and freshly ground black pepper

Make up the pastry and have it chilling in the fridge.

Prepare the filling by heating the stock in a medium-sized saucepan. Once it boils add the split peas, then cover and simmer gently for 10 minutes. Uncover and add the lentils then re-cover and continue to cook gently for 30 minutes or until the pulses are soft and all the liquid has been absorbed. Meanwhile in a separate, larger pan, heat the oil. Stir in the vegetables, herbs and garlic, cover and cook for 15 minutes until the vegetables are softened but not coloured. Pour the combined lentil and pea mixture into the vegetable pan and stir vigorously. Beat in the parsley and the majority of the egg, reserving just enough for the glaze. Taste and season if necessary.

Heat the oven to 220°C (425°F/Mark 7).

Have ready a greased baking sheet 32.5 cm (13 in) in length.

Roll out the pastry to a rectangle 30 × 27 cm (12 × 10½ in). Transfer to the baking sheet, then pile the vegetable mixture down the centre in a band about 8 cm (3 in) wide, leaving a gap of about 5 cm (2 in) at each end. Make diagonal cuts down the long sides of the pastry at 2.5-cm (1-in) intervals. Fold in the two ends. Drawing alternate strips from each side, work down the length, enclosing the filling in a pastry plait. Glaze with the reserved beaten egg. Bake in the centre of the oven for 30 to 35 minutes or until browned and crisp. Serve warm with yogurt or home-made tomato sauce.

Italian-Style Ricotta Tart
with Almond Pastry

This is rather like a cheesecake in texture and has a good flavour. It is best served warm or at room temperature; if refrigerated the texture becomes too dense and solid.

Pastry

75 g (3 oz) unblanched almonds
2 tablespoons Demerara sugar
175 g (6 oz) 85% plain brown flour
75 g (3 oz) vegetable margarine
1 egg white, lightly beaten

MAKES 6 OR 12 SLICES

Filling

350 g (12 oz) ricotta cheese
3 tablespoons double cream
2 tablespoons honey
2 eggs, beaten
2 tablespoons unblanched almonds, cut into slivers
2 tablespoons pine nuts
1 tablespoon Kirsch
1 tablespoon Grand Marnier
Grated rind of 1 orange and 1 lemon

Heat the oven to 190°C (375°F/Mark 5).

Put a baking sheet to heat in the oven. You will also need a round, sloping-sided pie tin measuring 4 cm (1½ in) deep, base 18 cm (7 in), top 24 cm (9½ in).

Use a liquidizer or food processor to reduce the nuts and sugar to a fine meal. Put into a bowl with the flour and margarine. Rub the fat into the dry ingredients, then add sufficient lightly beaten egg white to bring the mix together to form an unsticky dough. Weigh and reserve 110 g (4 oz) of the made dough. Roll out the rest and use to line the pie tin. Prick the base well with a fork and bake on the baking sheet for 20 minutes.

Meanwhile prepare the filling. Sieve the ricotta cheese into a mixing bowl and stir in the rest of the ingredients, one by one, in the order given above.

Remove the tart shell from the oven and leave to cool whilst rolling out the reserved 110-g (4-oz) piece of dough. Roll the dough to a rectangle 20 cm (8 in) long; cut into 10 strips 20 cm (8 in) long and about ½ cm (¼ in) wide. Spoon the filling into the tart shell and smooth the top. Lay the strips over the surface, five, regularly spaced, straight across the pie, the other five, similarly spaced, at right-angles, to achieve a lattice-work effect. Cut off the excess strip ends. (There is no need to dampen and stick the ends in any way.) Return the tart to bake on the baking sheet at the same temperature for about 1 hour. The tart is cooked when puffed and golden. Serve with cream or a thin apple purée.

Wholefood Roly-Poly

Done in just the same way as the old-fashioned jam roly-poly but made with grated vegetable margarine instead of suet. It can be sweet or savoury, see alternative fillings below.

Pastry
225 g (8 oz) 85% self-raising brown flour
110 g (4 oz) Tomor kosher margarine, frozen
about 8 tablespoons water

Filling (sweet)
225 g (8 oz) mixed dried fruit, soaked overnight
50 g (2 oz) chopped walnuts
25 g (1 oz) dark, soft brown sugar

Filling (savoury)
110 g (4 oz) thinly sliced button mushrooms
½ medium-sized onion, thinly sliced
either 110 g (4 oz) unsmoked bacon rashers,
  rinded and cut across into strips
or 110 g (4 oz) thinly sliced Cheddar cheese
2 tablespoons chopped parsley

MAKES 8-9 SLICES

Heat the oven to 180°C (350°F/Mark 4).

To make the pastry, have the flour ready in a bowl. Wrap the block of weighed margarine in sufficient foil or greaseproof paper to hold it. Dip the end in the flour and grate a little, stopping to toss this in the flour. Carry on in this manner until all the margarine has been grated. Combine the mixture with sufficient water to form a soft but not sticky dough. Wrap in cling film and chill whilst the filling is prepared.

Sweet filling Position a sieve over a bowl and pour in the fruit and soaking juices. When drained chop the fruit, removing the stones from the prunes as you work. Reserve the soaking liquor.

Roll out the pastry on a floured work surface to a rectangle approximately 40.5 × 23 cm (18 × 9 in). Spread the chopped fruit onto the pastry leaving a clear border of 2.5 cm (1 in) all round the edge. Sprinkle on the walnuts and sugar, then fold in the edge all round. Roll up from the short end, Swiss-roll style. Transfer to a sheet of foil and make a neat but loose parcel to allow room for expansion during baking. Bake on a baking sheet for one hour, then open up the foil parcel. Increase the oven temperature to 200°C (400°F/Mark 6) and bake for a further 15 to 20 minutes. Serve hot, sliced, with the warmed soaking liquor from the dried fruit and/or custard.

Savoury filling Follow the instructions for rolling out the pastry as above. Spread the filling ingredients over the pastry leaving a clear border as described above. The rolling, wrapping and baking are also the same. Serve the roll hot, sliced with a simple home-made tomato sauce (see the recipe for tomato sauce in Finnish-Style Pancakes page 83, but omit the chilli).

Individual Curd Cheese Cakes

These are rather lovely, but as with many a baked cheese cake, they rise in the baking and fall on cooling. This is absolutely normal and gives them their characteristic 'hills and hollows' appearance.

Pastry
Quick Wholewheat Flaky Pastry (see method on
   page 59) made with
     175 g (6 oz) 100% plain wholewheat flour
     125 g (4½ oz) Tomor kosher margarine,
       frozen hard
     5-6 tablespoons cold water, to mix

SERVES 24

Filling
125 g (4½ oz) vegetable margarine
125 g (4½ oz) light, soft brown sugar
2 size 2 eggs, beaten
75 g (3 oz) dry plain sponge cake crumbs
75 g (3 oz) currants
175 g (6 oz) curd cheese
grated rind of ½ lemon
¼ nutmeg, freshly grated

Have the pastry wrapped and chilling in the fridge.

You will need two 12-hole patty tins, lightly greased.

Heat the oven to 200°C (400°F/Mark 6).

Roll out the pastry to a large round about 3 mm (⅛ in) thick. Use an 8.5-cm (3¼-in) fluted cutter to stamp out 24 rounds. (You will need to re-roll the pastry trimmings to get this number.) Ease the rounds gently into the patty tins.

To make the filling beat the margarine and sugar together. Gradually add the beaten egg, a little at a time, beating well between each addition. As soon as the mixture looks as though it can take no more egg without curdling, fold in the cake crumbs before adding the remaining egg and the rest of the ingredients. Spoon this into the pastry cases and bake in the centre of the oven until puffed and brown. Leave to cool in the trays for 5 minutes before removing to a wire rack to cool.

BATTERS, SCONES AND MUFFINS

Basic Wholewheat Pancakes

Pancakes are comparatively easy if you have a good, well-seasoned pan to cook them in. It is best to have one iron pan which is kept aside solely for frying pancakes. This never gets washed, but is simply heated and oiled. If pancakes tend to stick, then heat your pan with a sprinkling of salt in the base. Remove from the heat and, using a wad of kitchen paper, scour the pan thoroughly with the salt. Discard the salt and wipe the pan with a fresh sheet of kitchen paper. Do not wash it now or ever! It is now ready to use.

110 g (4 oz) wholewheat flour
2 size 2 eggs, beaten
275 ml (½ pint) mixed milk and water
2 tablespoons vegetable oil or melted vegetable
  margarine   MAKES 12

You will need an 18-cm (7-in) pan in which to fry the pancakes.

Put the flour in a mixing bowl and make a well in the centre. Pour in the egg and half the milk and water. Beat with a spoon, gradually incorporating the surrounding flour, until smooth. Gradually add the remaining milk/water, and the oil or melted margarine.

Heat the pan, then, using a wad of kitchen paper moistened with oil, wipe the oil around the inside of the pan. This is all the oil needed to grease the pan. You may prefer either to ladle the batter into the pan or pour it from a jug. Whichever method you adopt give the batter a good stir before pouring into the pan to prevent the coarser bits in the flour forming a sediment at the bottom. Pour the equivalent of about 2 tablespoons of batter into the pan. As soon as the batter hits the pan tilt and turn it to obtain a thin, even coating in the base of the pan. Leave for about 30 seconds before checking the underside. If nicely browned, use a palette knife to turn the pancake over. Stack the cooked pancakes on a sheet of greaseproof paper.

Storage

I find that I usually need only half the quantity of pancakes that a 275-ml (½-pint) batter gives and find it very useful to store the rest, in either the fridge or the freezer – a useful standby. To store in a fridge make sure the pancakes are cold before wrapping the stack in foil or putting in a plastic bag. They will keep for several days. To freeze them, interleave the pancakes with squares of oiled greaseproof paper, then put into a plastic bag, being careful to expel all the air before sealing. My experience is that they should not be frozen for much more than eight weeks.

Alternative Flavourings for the Basic Batter

These can be adapted according to the type of filling desired so the pancakes flavour and the filling complement each other.
Cheese Add 75 g (3 oz) grated cheese.
Onion Add 2 tablespoons finely chopped spring onions or 1 tablespoon grated onion.
Chopped fresh herbs Some of the stronger herbs are ideal, e.g., rosemary, thyme, sage. Add about 2 teaspoons of the freshly chopped herb to the batter and leave aside for about 30 minutes for the flavour to develop. Stir the batter well before using.

Seeds Seeds such as caraway, anise and celery can be crushed slightly and added. Again, allow time for the flavour to develop.
Citrus rind The grated rind of an orange or lemon.
Carob Add 1 tablespoon carob powder to the batter.

Finnish-Style Spinach Pancakes with Sweetcorn

A good supper dish; the pancakes are served, two per person, sandwiched with a slightly chilli-hot sauce and grated Parmesan.

Pancakes	*Tomato sauce*
5 tablespoons 100% plain wholewheat flour	2 tablespoons vegetable oil
1 egg, plus 1 egg yolk	1 onion, chopped
2 tablespoons vegetable oil	¼ teaspoon crumbled, dried chilli peppers
1 teaspoon brown sugar	1 396-g (14-oz) can tomatoes
275 ml (½ pint) skimmed milk	2 teaspoons tomato purée
225 g (8 oz) trimmed spinach, washed	salt and freshly ground black pepper
2 spring onions, finely chopped	about 75 g (3 oz) grated Parmesan
150 g (5 oz) sweetcorn kernels	
freshly grated nutmeg	
salt and freshly ground black pepper	SERVES 3 (MAKES 6 PANCAKES)

You will need a small frying pan with a base no more than 15 cm (6 in) diameter. (In a larger pan, the pancakes are difficult to turn.)

Prepare the pancake batter. Put the flour, egg and yolk, oil and sugar into a bowl; gradually add the milk to obtain a thin, lump-free batter.

Put the wet spinach leaves into a saucepan, cover and cook for about 5 minutes, stirring occasionally until all the leaves are wilted. Drain in a colander and squeeze out the excess liquid. Chop coarsely and add to the batter with the spring onions and sweetcorn kernels. Taste and add freshly grated nutmeg and a little salt and freshly ground black pepper as desired. Cover and leave aside for 30 minutes.

To make the sauce, gently fry the onion in the oil for 5 minutes without allowing it to brown. Add the chillies and the tomatoes. Bring to simmering point and cook for 20 minutes. Liquidize or whizz in a food processor very briefly so the sauce still has a lot of texture. Return to the saucepan, stir in the tomato purée and season to taste. Keep hot.

Heat the frying pan, then wipe a wad of kitchen paper, moistened with oil, around the inside of the pan. Pour a ladleful of the batter into the pan and cook over a low heat until well-browned on the underside and set on the surface. Turn with the aid of a palette knife and cook the other side. These pancakes will take about 3 to 4 minutes on each side. Turn the cooked pancake onto a warmed plate. Make the remaining pancakes in the same way. Spread three of the pancakes with some of the hot sauce and sprinkle with Parmesan. Cover with another pancake, sprinkle this with additional Parmesan. Serve hot, garnished with watercress, if liked.

Cornmeal Pancakes with Spinach, Tuna and Caper Filling

A pleasant-textured pancake, thanks to the cornmeal. Like me, you might find it easier to work with a ladle when scooping the batter into the pan but the most important thing is to keep giving the batter a good stir otherwise the cornmeal forms a sediment. These pancakes are cooked only on one side, which means you can get through the cooking fairly quickly. It works – you will see!

Pancakes
170 ml (6 fl oz) skimmed milk
50 g (2 oz) coarse cornmeal
3 tablespoons 85% plain brown flour
1 egg
2 teaspoons vegetable oil
salt and freshly ground black pepper
freshly grated nutmeg

Filling
450 g (1 lb) trimmed spinach, well washed
1 medium-sized onion, finely chopped
1 170-g (6-oz) can tuna fish in oil
2 tablespoons capers, drained and chopped
2-3 teaspoons lemon juice

Sauce
3 medium-sized tomatoes (weighing about
   300 g (11 oz) altogether), skinned and
   chopped
1 fat clove garlic, sliced in half
½ teaspoon sugar

Topping
25 g (1 oz) grated Parmesan cheese

MAKES ABOUT 6 PANCAKES

Make the sauce first to allow it time to develop a subtle garlic flavour. Put the chopped tomatoes in a bowl with the sliced garlic, sugar and a little seasoning to taste. Cover and leave aside.

Then prepare the filling. Pack the washed, wet spinach into a large saucepan, cover and cook over a moderate heat for 5 minutes, stirring once or twice. When all the leaves have wilted, drain them in a colander. As soon as they are cool enough to handle, squeeze the leaves to get rid of excess water, then chop them. Using the oil from the can of tuna gently fry the chopped onion until softened and golden. Turn off the heat and stir in the chopped spinach, tuna fish, capers, lemon and salt and pepper to taste.

Make the pancakes by combining the ingredients together in a bowl in the order given. Heat a pancake pan, brush with a little oil, give the batter a good stir and spoon in just sufficient to cover the base of the pan, twisting and tilting it as soon as the batter is added. Cook until golden brown on the base, then turn out onto kitchen paper *uncooked side up*. Repeat with the remaining batter, remembering to stir well before spooning it into the pan. Roll an equal quantity of the spinach and tuna filling in each pancake and place (browned side out) in a fireproof rectangular serving dish. Remove the garlic from the sauce and pour it over the pancakes. Sprinkle the whole with Parmesan cheese. Grill or bake until hot right through.

Buckwheat Pancakes with Curried Chicken Filling (top left)
Cornmeal Pancakes with Spinach, Tuna and Caper Filling (top right)
Yeast Pancakes with Chicken and Avocado Filling (centre and bottom right)
Finnish-Style Spinach Pancakes with Sweetcorn (bottom left)

Buckwheat Pancakes with
Curried Chicken Filling

A beautifully-behaved batter that produces lovely cellular pancakes.

Pancakes

150 g (5 oz) buckwheat flour
110 g (4 oz) 100% plain wholewheat flour
570 ml (1 pint) skimmed milk
4 tablespoons vegetable margarine
4 eggs
vegetable oil for frying   MAKES ABOUT 20

Filling

1 medium-sized onion, finely chopped
4 tablespoons vegetable oil
1 tablespoon hot madras curry powder
2 tablespoons wholewheat flour
425 ml (¾ pint) chicken stock
2 chicken breasts, boned, skinned and cut into
    1-cm (½-in) cubes
½ cucumber
6 tablespoons yogurt
1 scant tablespoon home-made chutney   FILLS ABOUT 6 PANCAKES

To make the pancakes combine the flours together in a bowl. In a saucepan warm the milk and margarine just sufficiently to melt the fat, then remove from the heat and leave to cool to about blood temperature. Whisk the eggs into the milk, then incorporate this liquid gradually into the flour to form a smooth batter. Leave to stand for 30 minutes. Use an 18-cm (7-in) base pan to fry the pancakes in the usual way. (If in doubt see instructions for Basic Wholewheat Pancakes on page 82.) Stack the cooked pancakes on a sheet of greaseproof paper.

To make the filling heat 2 tablespoons of oil in a medium-sized saucepan and gently fry the onion for 10 minutes without browning. Remove the pan from the heat and stir in the curry powder and flour. Gradually stir in the stock, then return the pan to the heat and bring to the boil, stirring. Leave the sauce to boil gently, uncovered, for 8 to 10 minutes until reduced to slightly less than 275 ml (½ pint). Leave aside, off the heat. In a frying pan heat the remaining oil and briskly fry the chicken in several batches until golden brown; remove to a plate. Peel half a cucumber, then use the peeler to remove broad bands of the cucumber – about 24 strips. Cut the bands in half lengthwise and across. Add these to the frying pan, again stirring over a brisk heat. Reheat the sauce, add the chicken pieces and the cucumber strips. As soon as the mixture boils remove from the heat and stir in the chutney followed by the yogurt. If serving immediately, quickly divide the filling between six pancakes, roll up and serve in a heated serving dish, or having filled the pancakes, transfer them to a buttered, ovenproof dish, cover with foil and heat through in the oven at 180°C (350°F/Mark 4) for 30 minutes. Serve hot with a chicory, orange and watercress salad or stir-fried beansprouts.

Yeast Pancakes with Chicken and Avocado Filling

These are thicker pancakes, but not at all chewy. They have a pleasant flavour and their only drawback seems to be that they do not freeze well.

Pancakes
2 teaspoons dried yeast
1 teaspoon Muscovado sugar
225 g (8 oz) 100% plain wholewheat flour
½ teaspoon fine sea salt
1 tablespoon vegetable oil
1 egg, lightly beaten
150 ml (¼ pint) skimmed milk

MAKES 12

Filling
25 g (1 oz) vegetable margarine
25 g (1 oz) brown flour
150 ml (¼ pint) skimmed milk
150 ml (¼ pint) chicken stock
1 tablespoon dry sherry
1-2 teaspoons lemon juice
salt and freshly ground black pepper
225 g (8 oz) cooked chicken, chopped
1 avocado, skinned and cubed
1-2 oz grated Wensleydale cheese

ENOUGH FOR 6 PANCAKES

In a small bowl combine 275 ml (½ pint) hand-hot water with the sugar. Using a fork, whisk in the dried yeast and then leave aside for 15 minutes until frothy.

Meanwhile combine the flour and salt in a mixing bowl. Pour in the yeast liquid, followed by the oil and beaten egg. Mix well to form a smooth mixture, then cover and leave in a warm place for 30 minutes to develop a thick mousse-like consistency. Stir in the skimmed milk. Use a frying pan with an 18-cm (7-in) base. Heat the pan, then, using a wad of kitchen paper moistened with vegetable oil, wipe the oil around the inside of the pan. Spoon in about 2 tablespoons batter, instantly tilt the pan so the base gets an even coating of batter. After about half a minute check the underside, if nicely browned use a palette knife to turn and cook on the other side. Stack the pancakes on a greaseproof sheet as they are cooked.

For the filling heat the margarine in a medium-sized saucepan. When melted, stir in the flour. Remove the pan from the heat and gradually incorporate the milk and stock. Bring to the boil, stirring, then boil gently for 2 minutes. Remove from the heat and add the sherry and lemon juice and seasonings to your taste, then stir in the chicken and avocado. Reheat briefly, then spoon onto the pancakes, roll up and arrange in a fireproof rectangular buttered dish. Sprinkle with cheese, then cook under a moderately heated grill until everything is well heated through and the cheese melted and lightly browned.

Boozey Pancakes

These make a definitely beery-tasting pancake which seems to marry up best with well-flavoured fruits like Cox's apples or dried apricots, or for savoury fillings, cheese, bacon and onions. The quantity given below makes about 18 pancakes. It is unlikely that you will need this quantity at one sitting, but I decided to stick with this recipe as it was because pancakes freeze so readily and are a very useful standby. I make the full quantity and freeze what doesn't get eaten.

Pancakes
225 ml (8 fl oz) skimmed milk
110 g (4 oz) 85% plain brown flour
50 g (2 oz) 100% plain wholewheat flour
3 eggs
1 teaspoon Muscovado sugar
¼ teaspoon fine sea salt
150 ml (¼ pint) stout
a little oil for frying

Filling (enough for 7-8 pancakes)
350 g (12 oz) dried apricots
2 large bananas, coarsely chopped
2 tablespoons Kirsch
1 tablespoon lemon juice

Put all the ingredients except the beer into a processor or liquidizer and blend until smooth. Alternatively, put the dry ingredients into a bowl and make a well in the centre. Into this break the eggs and pour in the milk. Using a wire whisk, beat, gradually incorporating the dry ingredients until a smooth batter is formed. Leave aside for 1 hour. When ready to make the pancakes (not before!) add the beer. Use a frying pan with an 18-cm (7-in) base. Heat the pan, then using a wad of kitchen paper, moistened with vegetable oil, wipe the oil around the inside of the pan. Heat the pan over a moderate heat and spoon in about 2 tablespoons of batter, tipping the pan all the while so the base gets a thin, even coating of batter. After about a minute it will be ready to turn; cook for another half-minute, then turn out onto a warmed plate. Re-grease the pan in the same fashion and repeat until all the batter has been used. The pancakes can be filled as desired or try the filling below.

Put the dried apricots into a small saucepan with 275 ml (½ pint) water. Bring to the boil, then reduce to a simmer, cover and cook for 10 minutes or until plump and tender. Boil until about 1 tablespoon of free liquid is left in the pan; mash or coarsely chop the apricots, then mix in the remaining ingredients. The filling can be heated through and as the pancakes are cooked, 1-2 tablespoons of the apricot mix can be rolled up in each one and served. Otherwise make all the pancakes, roll a little filling into 7 or 8 of them, then line them up in a buttered rectangular ovenproof dish. Cover closely with foil and bake at 150°C (360°F/Mark 2) for 30 minutes. Serve hot with whipped cream and chopped walnuts or, if you would prefer to avoid cream, pour over orange juice concentrate which has been heated and slightly diluted.

Banana and Orange Clafoutis

Very simple – a good, last-minute type of pudding. A clafoutis might be described as a sweet, softer, creamier version of toad-in-the-hole.

5 tablespoons light, soft brown sugar
3 bananas
275 ml (½ pint) fresh half-cream (12%
*   butterfat)*
150 ml (¼ pint) skimmed milk
3 eggs, beaten
40 g (1½ oz) 85% plain brown flour
grated rind of 1 orange
1 teaspoon natural vanilla essence   SERVES 6

Heat the oven to 190°C (375°F/Mark 5).
    Select a roasting tin, 9 × 7 in (23 × 18 cm).
    Sprinkle 2 tablespoons of the sugar in the base. Peel the bananas and cut each into three. Combine the remaining sugar with the rest of the ingredients and beat together until smooth. Pour the batter over the bananas and bake in the top third of the oven for 45 to 50 minutes until the batter is lightly set and golden brown around the edge. Serve warm.

Honeyed Orange Waffles

Waffles are always very good as a stopgap; quickly made and filling. In an effort to try and bypass serving the usual syrup and butter with these waffles, try thawed, concentrated orange juice, thinned with a little Grand Marnier. Another alternative you might like to try is sprinkling a tablespoon of chopped nuts on before cooking each waffle.

3 eggs, separated
240 ml (8 fl oz) skimmed milk
120 ml (4 fl oz) vegetable oil
grated rind and juice of 1 large orange
2 tablespoons honey
275 g (10 oz) 85% plain brown flour
1 tablespoon baking powder   MAKES 10

Put the egg yolks in a mixing bowl and whisk in the milk, oil, orange rind and juice and honey. Stir in the flour and baking powder. With a clean, dry whisk, beat the egg whites in a separate bowl until stiff but not dry. Using a large metal spoon fold the whites into the batter mixture.
    Heat the waffle iron, lightly brush with oil and pour about 2 large spoonfuls of batter onto the centre of the waffle iron. Sprinkle with chopped nuts if liked. Cook and serve hot. See serving suggestion above.

American-Style Wholewheat Flapjacks

Flapjacks are the American name for our Scotch pancakes or drop scones. Serve hot with maple syrup or honey, and butter (yes, in this instance I definitely prefer butter) or with soured cream and home-made damson jam – if you happen to have some around – delicious!

110 g (4 oz) 100% plain wholewheat flour
50 g (2 oz) 85% plain brown flour
25 g (1 oz) wheatgerm
1 tablespoon dark, soft brown sugar
1 teaspoon baking powder
¼ teaspoon bicarbonate of soda
1 egg
150 ml (¼ pint) yogurt
150 ml (¼ pint) skimmed milk
1 tablespoon vegetable oil   MAKES 10

Ideally, these would be cooked on a griddle, the heavier the better because this means it will have a good, uniform heat. If you do not possess this piece of equipment, then a good, solid frying pan will do. Have the griddle or pan heating (unoiled) over a low heat whilst preparing the batter.

Put all the dry ingredients together in a mixing bowl. Rub the sugar into the mixture much as you would rub the fat into flour for pastry.

In a separate bowl whisk together the egg, yogurt, skimmed milk and oil. Add this to the dry ingredients all in one go and stir to form a batter. Turn the heat up a little under the pan and grease it, using a wad of kitchen paper moistened with vegetable oil. Ladle enough batter onto the pan to form a round about 10 cm (4 in) in diameter. If the batter seems too thick, add up to 2 tablespoons more milk; more than this should not be necessary. The amount needed depends on the thickness of the yogurt so it is difficult to be specific. As soon as the flapjack seems just set around the edge and no longer liquid on the surface, use a spatula to flip it over. It will probably be possible to cook three or four at a time without the pancakes running into one another. Serve hot on a warmed plate covered with a napkin.

Blackberry Drop Scones (top-left)
American-Style Wholewheat Flapjacks (top right)
Honeyed Orange Waffles (centre left)
Welsh Cakes with Mincemeat Filling (bottom right)
Banana and Orange Clafoutis (bottom left)

Blackberry Drop Scones

200 g (7 oz) self-raising brown flour   1 egg
25 g (1 oz) 100% wholewheat semolina   275 ml (½ pint) skimmed milk
50 g (2 oz) light, soft brown sugar   175 g (6 oz) fresh blackberries
½ teaspoon bicarbonate of soda
1 teaspoon cream of tartar   MAKES 14

You will need either a griddle or a large, thick-based frying pan.

Put the dry ingredients into a bowl. Break in the egg and pour in a little of the milk. Mix using a balloon whisk, then gradually add the rest of the milk to the mixture to form a smooth batter.

Heat the griddle or pan over a moderate heat before wiping with a pad of kitchen paper moistened with oil. Have the blackberries alongside the cooker, ready to use. Pour spoonfuls of the batter onto the pan or griddle and immediately sprinkle a few of the blackberries onto the surface then press them down slightly. When bubbles rise to the surface of each pancake and the tops just start to set, use a palette knife to flip them over and carry on cooking until you are sure they are cooked through. Serve warm with a little butter and honey.

Welsh Cakes with Mincemeat Filling

With grateful thanks to Auntie Gwyneth.

225 g (8 oz) 85% self-raising brown flour   1 egg
½ teaspoon mixed spice   1-2 tablespoons skimmed milk
50 g (2 oz) dark, soft brown sugar   a little mincemeat
110 g (4 oz) vegetable margarine
50 g (2 oz) currants   MAKES 9

Mix the flour, spice and sugar together in a bowl. Rub in the fat until the mixture resembles breadcrumbs, then stir in the currants. In a cup whisk together the egg and milk with a fork. Pour onto the dry ingredients and stir to form a dough. Turn out onto a lightly floured surface, knead lightly and briefly and roll out to a round slightly less than 0.5 cm (¼ in) thick. Cut into rounds using a plain, round 7-cm (2¾-in) cutter. Dampen the edge of *half* the rounds with water. Put about a teaspoonful of mincemeat in the centre of each of these rounds, then cover with the remaining rounds, pressing them lightly around the edges to seal.

Heat a griddle iron or large, heavy-based frying pan. Using a wad of kitchen paper moistened with oil, lightly grease the base of the griddle iron or pan. The Welsh cakes can be cooked close together as they do not expand very much during cooking. Cook over a low heat checking that they are not browning too fast. They will take about 5 minutes on each side. Re-roll any dough trimmings while the first batch cooks. Serve warm or cold.

Note If you would prefer to make the more usual Welsh cakes, omit anything to do with mincemeat and add a further 25 g (1 oz) currants to the recipe. Roll out the dough to ½ cm (¼ in) thick and no less. These will take 3 minutes on each side to cook and this method will make about 20 Welsh cakes.

Honey, Currant and Bran Scones

175 g (6 oz) 85% plain brown flour
50 g (2 oz) 100% plain wholewheat flour
2 tablespoons bran flakes
1 tablespoon baking powder
½ teaspoon bicarbonate of soda
½ teaspoon salt
75 g (3 oz) vegetable margarine

50 g (2 oz) currants
2 eggs
2 tablespoons clear honey
2-3 tablespoons creamed smetana or
natural yogurt or buttermilk

MAKES 8 SLICES

Heat the oven to 200°C (400°F/Mark 6).

Measure the first six ingredients into a mixing bowl. Rub the margarine in until the mixture resembles breadcrumbs, then sprinkle in the currants. In a bowl whisk together the remaining ingredients until thoroughly mixed. Stir the liquid ingredients into the dry to form a soft dough.

Sprinkle the work surface with bran flakes before scooping the dough out onto it. Knead it briefly but lightly into a ball, then transfer to a baking sheet and pat it out to a round, about 20 cm (8 in) in diameter. Use a large kitchen knife to cut the dough into eighths, keeping it as a round. Bake in the top half of the oven for 20 minutes. Serve warm.

Walnut, Black Treacle and Yogurt Scones

These scones are not too sweet. If you don't find them sweet enough for your taste, serve just warm, with honey butter (i.e. honey beaten into butter).

225 g (8 oz) 85% plain brown flour
2 tablespoons light, soft brown sugar
1 tablespoon baking powder
½ teaspoon bicarbonate of soda
50 g (2 oz) vegetable margarine
75 g (3 oz) chopped walnuts

1 egg
2 tablespoons black treacle
5 tablespoons yogurt

MAKES 12

Heat the oven to 220°C (425°F/Mark 7).

Put the flour, sugar, baking powder and bicarbonate of soda into a bowl. Rub in the margarine until the mixture looks like ground almonds. Stir in the chopped walnuts.

In a separate bowl, whisk together the egg, treacle and yogurt with a fork. Stir into the flour and mix to form a soft dough. Turn out onto a floured surface, knead briefly and lightly, then pat out to a round 2 cm (¾ in) thick. Using a 5.5-cm (2¼-in) fluted cutter, cut out 12 rounds in all. Bake on an ungreased baking sheet on the second shelf from the top of the oven for 12 to 15 minutes. Serve warm.

Quick and Spicy Chelsea Buns

Not a yeast recipe, but one based on a scone mix, which explains its appearance in this section of the book. The result is, I think, quick, simple and effective.

Buns
110 g (4 oz) 100% plain wholewheat flour
110 g (4 oz) 85% plain brown flour
4 teaspoons baking powder
½ teaspoon salt
50 g (2 oz) vegetable margarine
150 ml (¼ pint) skimmed milk

Topping
3 teaspoons clear honey

Filling
50 g (2 oz) light, soft brown sugar
1 rounded teaspoon mixed spice
75 g (3 oz) currants
75 g (3 oz) vegetable margarine

MAKES 9

Heat the oven to 200°C (400°F/Mark 6).

Grease a shallow, square tin, measuring 18 × 18 × 3 cm (7 × 7 × 1¼ in).

Prepare the mixture for the filling by rubbing together the sugar and spice until no lumps of sugar remain. Stir in the currants, then put aside whilst preparing the scone dough.

Combine the flours, baking powder and salt in a bowl. Rub in the margarine until the mixture resembles fine breadcrumbs. Add all but one tablespoon of the measured milk and mix to a soft dough. Turn out onto a floured surface and knead very briefly and lightly. Roll out to an oblong 30 × 23 cm (12 × 9 in) and spread the top two-thirds of dough with half (i.e. 40 g/1½ oz) of the margarine to be used for the filling. Sprinkle half the spiced sugar over the margarine. Press it down lightly with the palm of the hand then fold up the dough, bringing the lower third over the central portion and folding the top third down over it. Press the open edges lightly with the rolling pin to seal them. Turn the dough so that the fold is on your left. Roll out again to the same dimensions, then spread all over with the remaining margarine and the rest of the spiced sugar mix. Roll up the dough Swiss-roll fashion from the long side. Cut into nine equal rounds and arrange in the tin in rows of three.

Bake in the centre of the oven for 30 minutes. Remove and leave to cool in the tin for 5 minutes before turning out. Drizzle the honey over the top of the buns and serve just warm. Like all scones these are best eaten as fresh as possible.

Oatmeal Scones with Mincemeat Waist (top left)
Walnut, Black Treacle and Yogurt Scones (top right)
Quick and Spicy Chelsea Buns (centre right)
Fresh Pear Scones (bottom right)
Honey, Currant and Bran Scones (bottom left)

Oatmeal Scones with Mincemeat Waist

These scones are made with sour milk. If none is available mix the milk with a teaspoon of lemon juice before adding the oatmeal.

225 g (8 oz) medium oatmeal
275 ml (½ pint) sour milk
225 g (8 oz) 85% plain brown flour
50 g (2 oz) vegetable margarine
25 g (1 oz) Muscovado sugar
1 teaspoon bicarbonate of soda
1 teaspoon cream of tartar
1 teaspoon salt
approximately 110 g (4 oz) mincemeat   MAKES 12

Combine the oatmeal and soured milk in a bowl; cover and leave aside for 1 hour.
  Heat the oven to 220°C (400°F/Mark 6).
  Measure all the remaining ingredients into a separate bowl. Rub the fat and sugar into the dry ingredients until the mixture resembles fine breadcrumbs. Stir this into the soaked oatmeal and mix to form a soft dough. Turn out onto a floured surface and pat out to a rectangle 30 × 20 cm (12 × 8 in). Spread mincemeat on half the long side, then with the aid of a fish slice or palette knife flip the other half of the dough over to cover the mincemeat. Now pat the rectangle a little flatter so it measures roughly 25.5 × 20 cm (10 × 6 in). Cut into 12 squares. Lift with a palette knife and transfer to baking sheets. Bake in the top half of the oven for 20 minutes. Serve hot.

Fresh Pear Scones

The flavour of cooked pears can be elusive, even when they are baked on their own; but I have found it comes across nicely in this recipe. By the way – don't bother to peel them unless you really prefer to. Because of the moisture in the fruit, these scones will still taste good the following day.

2 ripe pears
½ teaspoon lemon juice
about 4 tablespoons yogurt
225 g (8 oz) 85% plain brown flour
1 tablespoon light, soft brown sugar
1 tablespoon baking powder
½ teaspoon bicarbonate of soda
75 g (3 oz) vegetable margarine   MAKES 12

Heat the oven to 220°C (425°F/Mark 7).
  Have ready a lightly greased baking sheet.
  Quarter and core one pear. Liquidize with the lemon juice, then whisk in the yogurt.
  Put the dry ingredients into a bowl. Rub in the fat to give a uniform, fine crumb. Stir the pear purée into the dry ingredients to give a soft dough. Turn out onto a floured surface and pat out to a rectangle measuring approximately 20 × 30 cm (8 × 12 in).

Quarter, core and thinly slice the remaining pear onto half of one long side. Fold the other half over the top to give a pear 'sandwich'. Cut into 12 small squares. Place on the baking sheet and bake in the top half of the oven for 20 to 25 minutes. (These scones take longer to bake because of the moist pear centre.) Serve hot with honey.

Semolina and Cheddar Cheese Scones

This might sound a little odd to those people who associate semolina solely with the lumpy stuff that arrived with a red pond of jam in the middle for pudding at school. Here it gives a delicious light and crunchy texture to scones. Needless to say, it is not the refined variety used in the puddings of our childhood but 100% wholewheat semolina.

175 g (6 oz) 85% plain brown flour
75 g (3 oz) 100% semolina
4 teaspoons baking powder
½ teaspoon bicarbonate of soda
½ teaspoon salt
¼ teaspoon cayenne pepper
50 g (2 oz) vegetable margarine
2 tablespoons finely chopped spring onions
75 g (3 oz) grated Cheddar cheese
1 egg
150 ml (¼ pint) buttermilk
celery salt (optional)   MAKES 12

Heat the oven to 220°C (425°F/Mark 7).
   Have a baking sheet ready, lightly greased.
   In a mixing bowl combine the flour, semolina, baking powder, bicarbonate of soda, salt and cayenne pepper. Rub in the margarine until uniformly incorporated into the dry ingredients. Sprinkle in the chopped onion and grated cheese and stir gently to coat with flour.
   In a separate bowl whisk together the egg and buttermilk. Pour this onto the dry ingredients in one go and mix to form a soft dough. Lightly dust the work surface with semolina, turn out the dough and knead lightly for 2 or 3 turns. Pat out to a round 2 cm (¾ in) thick and use a 6-cm (2¼-in to 2½-in) plain round cutter to stamp out scones. Arrange on the baking sheet and sprinkle the tops with celery salt if liked. Bake in the top half of the oven for 15 to 20 minutes. Serve hot.

Malted Wheat Scones with Feta Cheese and Spring Onion

It is perfectly possible to find alternatives for any of the main ingredients in this recipe which you might have difficulty buying in your area. Wholewheat flour can be used instead of malted wheat flour; any medium fat soft cheese (but preferably one with a bit of a bite to it) can be used instead of Feta, and chives or 1 tablespoon grated onion could be used instead of spring onions. These are good picnic or lunchbox fare and go well with soups in winter.

225 g (8 oz) malted wheat flour
4 teaspoons baking powder
1 teaspoon salt
75 g (3 oz) Feta cheese
2 spring onions, finely chopped
about 150 ml (¼ pint) skimmed milk   MAKES 8

Heat the oven to 200°C (400°F/Mark 6).

In a mixing bowl combine the flour, baking powder and salt. Crumble the Feta cheese into the bowl, then rub into the dry ingredients exactly as you would rub fat into flour. Mix in the onions and stir in sufficient milk to form a soft dough. Turn the dough out onto a floured surface and knead very briefly and lightly to form the mixture into one large bun. Transfer this to a baking sheet and pat out to a round 18 to 20 cm (7 to 8 in) in diameter. Using a large knife, divide the round into eighths, retaining the round shape. Bake in the top half of the oven for 30 minutes or until browned and cooked in the centre. Eat warm or cold.

Semolina and Cheddar Cheese Scones (top)
Vegetable Gulyas with Cornmeal Scone Topping (bottom left)
Malted Wheat Scones with Feta Cheese and Spring Onion (bottom right)

Vegetable Gulyas with
Cornmeal Scone Topping

Here, the keyword is 'timing'. Of course, the vegetables I have used can be swapped around according to seasonal availability. But whatever is substituted, estimate how long it will take to cook and add it to the gulyas at the right stage. It should be a stew in which each piece of vegetable has its own discernible taste and a 'bite'. Then it is very good indeed.

Cornmeal scone topping

175 g (6 oz) 85% plain brown flour
75 g (3 oz) coarse cornmeal
25 g (1 oz) wheatgerm
1 tablespoon baking powder
¾ teaspoon bicarbonate of soda
½ teaspoon salt
75 g (3 oz) vegetable margarine
3 spring onions, finely chopped
150 ml (¼ pint) skimmed milk
2-3 tablespoons natural yogurt

SERVES 4-5

Gulyas

225 g (8 oz) small onions
225 g (8 oz) thumb-thick carrots
225 g (8 oz) string or young runner beans
2 stalks celery
225 g (8 oz) potatoes
225 g (8 oz) button mushrooms
2 peppers (1 green, 1 red if possible)
½ head cauliflower
3 tablespoons vegetable oil
2 tablespoons sweet paprika
2 tablespoons wholewheat flour
1 397-g (14-oz) can tomatoes (or 450 g/1 lb
  fresh, peeled tomatoes)
2 large cloves garlic, thinly sliced
2 bayleaves
275 ml (½ pint) vegetable stock
yogurt or soured cream, to serve

You will need a 3-litre (6-pint) ovenproof casserole.

Before preparing the scone topping halve the red pepper and discard the seeds. Grill one half, skin side up, until black (reserving the other half for the stew). Cool and strip off the skin, dice the flesh and reserve.

Put the first seven ingredients of the scone mix together in a bowl. Rub in the margarine until the mixture resembles coarse breadcrumbs. Sprinkle in the cooked, diced pepper and chopped spring onions, tossing them in the mixture with a fork. Stir in the milk and yogurt and mix to a soft dough. Turn out onto a floured surface and roll out to 1 cm (½ in) thick. Use a plain 4.5-cm (2½-in) cutter to stamp out 12 rounds.

When cutting up the vegetables it is better to keep them on the chunky side. Peel the onions and leave whole. Scrub the carrots and cut them into 2-cm (¾-in) lengths, cut the beans and celery in 2.5-cm (1-in) lengths. Scrub and cut the potatoes into 2.5-cm (1-in) cubes. Wipe and leave the mushrooms whole unless they are more than 3 cm (1½ in) in diameter in which case halve them. Halve, de-seed and cut peppers into postage-stamp-sized pieces. Trim the cauliflower down to florets, about the size of the mushrooms.

Heat the oven to 220°C (425°F/Mark 7).

Heat the oil in a large saucepan. Sauté the onions, carrots and celery over a fairly high heat in order to colour them. Turn down the heat, cover and cook for 5 minutes. Uncover, add the potatoes, mushrooms and pepper pieces. Again, sauté over a brisk heat to colour. Sprinkle in the paprika and flour and cook for a couple of minutes before adding the tomatoes, garlic and bayleaves.

Bring to the boil, stirring. Pour in the stock. Cover and cook gently for a further 5 minutes. Uncover, add the remaining vegetables. Bring to simmering point and taste and season with a little salt and some freshly ground black pepper. Transfer the vegetable mixture to a warmed casserole and arrange the scones, slightly overlapping, around the edge of the casserole. Bake the casserole in the top third of the oven for 20 minutes, then serve immediately with yogurt or soured cream.

Cranberry-Sharp Muffins

In late October or early November, fresh cranberries put in an appearance in greengrocers and supermarkets. I love them and use them in soups, sauces and desserts. If you have a food processor whizz them round briefly with the walnuts to save some chopping time.

50 g (2 oz) vegetable margarine
50 g (2 oz) dark, soft brown sugar
grated rind and juice of 1 medium-sized orange
1 egg
150 g (5 oz) 85% plain brown flour
110 g (4 oz) 100% plain wholewheat flour
1 tablespoon baking powder
170 ml (6 fl oz) skimmed milk
110 g (4 oz) fresh, coarsely chopped cranberries
50 g (2 oz) coarsely chopped walnuts   MAKES 12

Heat the oven to 200°C (400°F/Mark 6).

Use a deep 12-hole bun tin, each cup of 60-ml (4-tablespoon) capacity. Brush liberally with melted margarine.

In a mixing bowl cream the margarine and sugar together with the orange rind. In a separate bowl whisk the egg until frothy. Stir, do not beat, the egg into the creamed mix. Add the dry ingredients alternately with milk and orange juice, keeping the mixing to an absolute minimum. The mixture will probably be lumpy and look ghastly but this is exactly how it should be! Throw in the chopped cranberries and walnuts, stir twice and transfer the mixture to the greased tin. This quantity makes 12 exactly. Bake in the centre of the oven for 35 to 40 minutes by which time each muffin will have risen like a little volcano. Slip a knife around the inside edge of each cup to release the muffins. Turn out onto a wire rack and serve hot or cold.

Orange and Date Muffins

The great thing about muffins is speed. The faster you throw them together, the better they are.

1 small orange
200 g (7 oz) 85% plain brown flour
110 g (4 oz) light, soft brown sugar
25 g (1 oz) wheatgerm
1 teaspoon baking powder
1 teaspoon bicarbonate of soda
4 tablespoons orange juice
50 g (2 oz) vegetable margarine at room
  temperature
1 egg
75 g (3 oz) pitted dates   MAKES 12

Heat the oven to 200°C (400°F/Mark 6).

Use a deep 12-hole bun tin, each cup of 60-ml (4-tablespoon) capacity. Brush liberally with melted margarine.

Grate the orange rind into a mixing bowl and add the flour, sugar, wheatgerm, baking powder and bicarbonate of soda. Rub the sugar into the dry ingredients to break up any lumps. Peel the orange and separate into segments. If you have a food processor or liquidizer blend the de-pipped orange, orange juice, margarine, egg and dates for about 5 seconds, then pour onto the dry ingredients. If not, chop the orange segments (removing the pips) and the dates. Add to the dry ingredients with the orange juice, margarine and beaten egg. Once the wet ingredients meet the dry stir until *just* combined and *no more*. Spoon quickly into the muffin tins and bake in the centre of the oven for 15 to 20 minutes. Slip a knife around the inside edge of each muffin, then turn out onto a wire rack. Eat fresh.

Black-Bottom Bran Muffins

Very branny and very good. The 'black bottom' is a prune baked into the base of each muffin.

12 small or 6 large prunes, soaked overnight
25 g (1 oz) vegetable margarine
1-2 tablespoons Demerara sugar
60 g (2½ oz) bran flakes
50 g (2 oz) 85% plain brown flour
75 g (3 oz) 100% plain wholewheat flour
75 g (3 oz) chopped walnuts
1 teaspoon bicarbonate of soda
1 teaspoon cinnamon
1 teaspoon freshly grated nutmeg
1 teaspoon natural vanilla essence
1 egg, beaten
110 ml (4 fl oz) clear honey
175 ml (6 fl oz) skimmed milk
2 tablespoons vegetable oil

MAKES 12

Heat the oven to 190°C (375°F/Mark 5).

Use a deep, 12-hole bun tin, each cup of 60-ml (4-tablespoon) capacity. Put a flick of margarine in the base of each cup and place in the oven until the margarine has melted. Remove and brush the margarine around the sides of each cup, then sprinkle a little Demerara sugar in the bases. Drain the prunes.

Put all the ingredients except the prunes together in a bowl and stir just until thoroughly mixed. If using large prunes, cut in half, stone, and arrange a half in the base of each cup, cut side up; otherwise place a small prune in the base of each. Divide the mixture equally between the cups. Gently tap the tin on the work surface to settle the mixture, then bake in the centre of the oven for 15 to 20 minutes or until well risen and firm to the touch. Run a knife around the inside edge of each muffin before turning out onto a wire rack. Eat warm with butter, if liked. These muffins must be eaten fresh.

Apple Bran Muffins
Spiced with Cardamom

These muffins have only minimal sweetening and a lovely, spicy lemon flavour. In the recipe I have said that honey is spooned over the top of the piping hot muffins and they are then eaten with butter. But you can leave out the honey and eat them without butter for breakfast (or tea) and they are still very good!

75 g (3 oz) All Bran or similar cereal
275 g (½ pint) skimmed milk
1 large cooking apple
grated rind of 1 lemon
10 whole green cardamom pods
1 egg
3 tablespoons vegetable oil
2 tablespoons Muscovado sugar
75 g (3 oz) 100% plain wholewheat flour
75 g (3 oz) 85% plain brown flour
25 g (1 oz) wheatgerm
1 teaspoon baking powder
2-3 tablespoons clear honey   MAKES 12

Heat the oven to 200°C (400°F/Mark 6).

Use a deep, 12-hole bun tin, each cup of 60-ml (4-tablespoon) capacity. Brush liberally with melted margarine.

Sprinkle the bran cereal into a large bowl and pour on the milk. Stir and leave aside for 10 minutes to allow the cereal to absorb most of the milk.

Meanwhile, quarter and core the cooking apple. Reserve one quarter and finely chop or grate the remainder. Add to the cereal and milk followed by the grated lemon rind. Crush the cardamom pods, discard the pod casings and add the finely crushed seed to the bran mixture.

In a small bowl beat the egg and oil together followed by the sugar. When thoroughly mixed, stir into the bran mixture. Finally beat in the dry ingredients. When thoroughly combined, spoon the mixture into the prepared tin. (This quantity is enough to make 12 exactly.) Thinly slice the remaining apple quarter and push a slice into each bun so it pokes out of the top. Bake in the centre of the oven for 35 to 40 minutes or until well risen and browned on top. Drizzle a little honey over the top of each bun and serve hot. Pull apart, dab with butter and eat!

Cranberry-Sharp Muffins (top left)
Orange and Date Muffins (top right)
Apple Bran Muffins Spiced with Cardamom (bottom centre)
Black-Bottom Bran Muffins (bottom right)
Carob and Prune Muffins (bottom left)

Carob and Prune Muffins

110 g (4 oz) 85% plain brown flour
2 teaspoons baking powder
75 g (3 oz) dark, soft brown sugar
25 g (1 oz) carob or cocoa powder
2 eggs, separated
5 tablespoons skimmed milk
1 tablespoon oil
110 g (4 oz) ready-to-eat prunes, pitted and
  chopped
25 g (1 oz) sesame seeds   MAKES 10

Heat the oven to 200°C (400°F/Mark 6).

Use a deep, 12-hole bun tin, each cup of 60-ml (4-tablespoon) capacity. Brush liberally with melted margarine.

Combine the flour, baking powder, sugar and sifted carob powder together in a bowl. Rub the sugar into the dry ingredients to break up any lumps. In a separate small bowl, mix the egg yolks, milk and oil. Whisk together until frothy. Pour this onto the dry ingredients, add the chopped prunes and stir until thoroughly combined. Whisk the egg whites until stiff but not dry. Fold this into the carob/prune mixture, as lightly as possible. Spoon the mixture into the greased muffin cups (this quantity will make only 10), sprinkle with the sesame seeds and bake in the centre of the oven for 30 minutes.

Potato Sticks with Celery Seeds

These are good, simple nibbles to serve with drinks. The dough can be cut into any shape you like but I would advise pricking all but the stick shapes with a fork to prevent blistering.

75 g (3 oz) 100% plain wholewheat flour
75 g (3 oz) freshly boiled, sieved potato
50 g (2 oz) vegetable margarine
sea salt and freshly ground black pepper
a little beaten egg
celery seeds

Heat the oven to 180°C (350°F/Mark 4).

Have ready two baking sheets. It is not necessary to grease them.

Put the flour, sieved potato and margarine into a bowl with a fairly generous amount of freshly ground black pepper. Gradually work the ingredients together until they form a dough. Roll out the dough on a well-floured work surface to about 3 mm (⅛ in) thick. Brush the surface with the beaten egg and sprinkle with sea salt and celery seeds. Cut into sticks, or rounds, diamonds, rectangles – whatever you wish – and transfer to the baking sheets. Bake in the centre of the oven for 15 to 20 minutes, or until firm and golden. Cool on a wire rack before storing in an airtight container.

Bran and Parsley Biscuits

A slightly unusual cheese biscuit with a good flavour. Press hard when using the biscuit cutter, the bran flakes offer some resistance. When it comes to re-rolling the dough scraps, add a drop more milk to moisten.

175 g (6 oz) 100% plain wholewheat flour
50 g (2 oz) bran flakes
110 g (4 oz) vegetable margarine
1 teaspoon Muscovado sugar
1 teaspoon baking powder
½ teaspoon salt
freshly ground black pepper

a good handful parsley sprigs, finely chopped
2 spring onions, finely chopped
about 2 tablespoons milk

MAKES ABOUT 36

Heat the oven to 180°C (350°F/Mark 4).

Lightly grease two baking sheets.

Put the first seven ingredients into a bowl, then rub the margarine into the dry ingredients, taking care to see that the sugar is smoothly incorporated. When the mixture resembles coarse breadcrumbs add the parsley, onions and milk. Make it slightly more moist than you would for say, shortcrust pastry. Roll out on a lightly floured surface to 3 mm (⅛ in) thick. Use a plain 7-cm (2¾-in) cutter to cut out the biscuits. Arrange close together on the baking sheets and bake near the centre of the oven for 15 to 20 minutes or until the biscuits feel firm. Transfer to a wire rack to cook, then store in an airtight tin.

Peppery Cheese Biscuits

Cheese biscuits always taste good when spiked with something hot in the mixture. In the past I have used cayenne pepper and hot curry powder, here I have used freshly ground black pepper and found it simple and effective. I have given no indication as to how many biscuits this quantity will make because they can be made in a great variety of shapes. It is a recipe straightforward enough for children to tackle, or it can be reduced to a very simple procedure, for speed. The different techniques are given below.

75 g (3 oz) vegetable margarine
75 g (3 oz) freshly grated Parmesan
75 g (3 oz) 85% plain brown flour
½ teaspoon salt
¾-1 teaspoon freshly ground black pepper
poppy seeds

Heat the oven to 180°C (350°F/Mark 4).

Lightly grease two baking sheets.

In a bowl beat the margarine and cheese together. Add the flour, salt and freshly ground black pepper and work with a wooden spoon until the mixture comes together to form a fairly firm dough. Children could now form the dough into balls, slightly larger than marble size, roll these in poppy seeds, then put on the baking sheets (spacing is not important because they spread very little during baking) and flatten slightly. Or the dough can be rolled out to 3 mm (¼ in) thick and cut out with a biscuit cutter of whatever the desired size and shape. A particularly speedy method is to roll out the ball of dough on a *flat* baking sheet (or if your baking sheets all have some edge to them, turn them over and roll out the dough on the reverse side), sprinkle with poppy seeds, then cut the dough into squares or rectangles with a large knife and bake in the centre of the oven for 15 to 20 minutes. The biscuits baked *en bloc* will then need cutting into individual shapes along the previous cut marks. Cool on a wire rack and store in an airtight tin.

Wholewheat Oatcakes

It probably sounds strange for so basic a recipe, but the making and baking of oatcakes requires a fair degree of deftness. They can be baked in two ways. If you have a griddle or a large frying pan about 28 cm (11 in) in diameter the oatcakes can be baked on this in about 10 minutes. Or, slightly easier, bake in the oven at 150°C (300°F/Mark 2) for about an hour (perhaps whilst you have a casserole cooking). If you get the knack of managing oatcakes, you might like to try introducing freshly chopped herbs into the dough, e.g., rosemary, sage, thyme – the sort of flavours that complement cheese.

175 g (6 oz) 100% plain wholewheat flour
175 g (6 oz) medium oatmeal
1 teaspoon salt
¼ teaspoon bicarbonate of soda
75 g (3 oz) vegetable margarine   MAKES 8-10

Put the dry ingredients into a bowl and rub in the margarine. Mix to a soft but not sticky dough with about 2 tablespoons water. Divide the dough in half and roll out to 25.5 to 28 cm (10 to 11 in) in diameter. The dough can now be either cut out with a plain biscuit cutter or left as a round and divided into eight sections. Either transfer to a heated oiled griddle or bake in the oven as detailed above. Cool and store in an airtight container.

Wholewheat Oatcakes (top left)
Wholewheat and Oatmeal Digestives (top right)
Bran and Parsley Biscuits (centre)
Potato Sticks with Celery Seeds (bottom left)
Peppery Cheese Biscuits (bottom right)

111

Wholewheat and Oatmeal Digestives

These fall between being a sweet and being a savoury biscuit, and so can be eaten with a cup of coffee, or served with cheese; they are good either way. The toppings can be varied according to taste. Here I have used sesame seeds, but poppy seeds, bran flakes and cracked wheat are some of the alternatives.

175 g (6 oz) 100% plain, wholewheat flour
25 g (1 oz) 85% plain brown flour
25 g (1 oz) fine oatmeal
25 g (1 oz) Muscovado sugar
1 teaspoon baking powder
½ teaspoon salt
75 g (3 oz) vegetable margarine
2-3 tablespoons skimmed milk, to bind
1 tablespoon sesame seeds   MAKES 20

Heat the oven to 190°C (375°F/Mark 5).

You will need two baking sheets; it is not necessary to grease them.

Put the first six, dry ingredients into a mixing bowl and rub in the Muscovado sugar to break up any lumps. Add the margarine and rub this in as well until you get a fine, even crumb. Stir in sufficient milk to bring the mixture together to a firm dough. Transfer this to a lightly floured surface, knead briefly to a smooth round and roll out until 3 mm to ½ cm (⅛ to ¼ in) thick. Strew the surface with sesame seeds and run the rolling pin backwards and forwards over the dough once or twice. Use a plain 7-cm (2¾-in) cutter to cut out the rounds. Place on the baking sheets and bake in the oven for 15 to 20 minutes or until firm to the touch. Cool on a wire rack and store in an airtight container.

Cinnamon Sugar Kidney Biscuits

Biscuits
225 g (8 oz) vegetable margarine
50 g (2 oz) light, soft brown sugar
75 g (3 oz) unskinned, finely ground almonds
200 g (7 oz) 85% plain brown flour
50 g (2 oz) wheatgerm

Coating
75 g (3 oz) Muscovado sugar
2 tablespoons wheatgerm
3 teaspoons cinnamon

MAKES ABOUT 28

Heat the oven to 170°C (325°F/Mark 3).

Lightly grease two baking sheets.

Put all the ingredients for the biscuit mix together in one bowl and mix to a soft dough. Pinch off a little of the dough at a time, enough to form a finger-thick roll about 5 cm (2 in) long. Bend the ends round to form a crescent. Bake for 20 to 25 minutes until firm to touch.

While the biscuits are baking put all the ingredients for the coating in a plastic bag and mix well.

When the biscuits are baked give them a minute to cool and firm up a little, then pop them one at a time into the plastic bag. Push the sugar coating gently onto each biscuit. Shake a little and place on a wire rack to cool. Store in an airtight container when cold.

Oaty Thins

Again, a biscuit that is child's play to make. A sort of cut-and-come-again biscuit. The dough can be kept in the fridge and a tray of biscuits quickly cut and baked whenever the oven is on for some other purpose.

200 g (7 oz) light, soft brown sugar
110 g (4 oz) 100% plain wholewheat flour
½ teaspoon bicarbonate of soda
110 g (4 oz) vegetable margarine
1 egg
75 g (3 oz) rolled oats

MAKES ABOUT 40

Heat the oven to 200°C (400°F/Mark 6).

Put all the ingredients in a bowl. Start mixing with a spoon, then use your hand to work everything gradually together to form a dough. Refrigerate the mixture for 30 minutes then remove and form the dough into a uniform roll, about 4 cm (1½ in) in diameter. I usually put the dough onto a standard-sized sheet of greaseproof paper and work the dough into a sausage shape the width of the paper. I then roll it up completely in the paper and leave it to firm up again in the fridge.

When ready, cut the roll into very thin slices, no more than 3 cm (⅛ in), and arrange on greased baking sheets. Bake in the centre of the oven for 7 or 8 minutes or until the edges of the biscuits are just beginning to darken. Remove from the oven and leave to cool and firm up for 3 or 4 minutes before easing the biscuits off the baking sheets using a metal spatula. Transfer to a cooling rack and when cold, store in an airtight container.

Freezer Lemon and Cardamom Biscuits

Lovely, crisp-crunchy and lemon-spicy. This sort of cut-and-come-again biscuit is very useful. The dough can be stored in the form of a roll, ready to slice, for up to 10 days in a fridge or six months in a freezer. Leave the dough overnight in the fridge to defrost, then slice and bake.

Biscuits
110 g (4 oz) vegetable margarine
200 g (7 oz) light, soft brown sugar
grated rind of 1 lemon
1 egg
1 tablespoon lemon juice
200 g (7 oz) 85% plain brown flour
2 tablespoons brown rice flour or 100%
  semolina
2 tablespoons bran flakes
12 green cardamom pods

Coating
about 50 g (2 oz) bran flakes   MAKES 36

Heat the oven to 180°C (350°F/Mark 4).

In a mixing bowl combine the margarine, sugar and grated lemon rind. Beat until paler in colour. Then beat in the egg thoroughly before adding the lemon juice. Stir in the plain flour, rice flour and bran flakes. Crush the cardamom pods using a pestle and mortar. When the seeds are freed, discard the pods and carry on crushing the remaining black seeds until they resemble finely ground black pepper. Stir this thoroughly into the biscuit mixture. Cover the bowl and chill in the fridge for an hour.

Sprinkle the bran flakes onto a sheet of greaseproof paper. Transfer the chilled biscuit mix to the paper and shape into a roll measuring 20 × 5 cm (8 × 2 in). Roll up in the greaseproof paper and chill again until firm (or freeze for future use). Cut into slices 5 mm (¼ in) thick using a scallop-edged knife and arrange on a greased baking sheet allowing about 2.5 cm (1 in) around each biscuit for expansion during baking. Bake for 15 to 20 minutes or until biscuits are just firm in the centre and tinged brown around the edge. Allow 2 or 3 minutes to firm up before removing from the baking sheet using a flexible metal palette knife. If they become too cold and stick firmly to the baking sheet, return them to the oven for 2 or 3 minutes, then they should be easily removed.

Maximum Crunch Biscuits (top left)
Hermits (top right)
Peanut and Molasses Munchies (below top dish)
Freezer Lemon and Cardamom Biscuits (right of Munchies)
Oaty Thins (below Munchies)
Honey and Apricot Shortbread (bottom left)
Cinnamon Sugar Kidney Biscuits (bottom right)

Peanut and Molasses Munchies

These are good as long as you enjoy the flavour of molasses (or substitute with black treacle); because I realize it is something of an acquired taste.

Biscuits
110 g (4 oz) shelled, unsalted peanuts, finely
    chopped
175 g (6 oz) vegetable margarine
225 g (8 oz) dark, soft brown sugar
1 egg
5 tablespoons molasses
225 g (8 oz) 85% plain brown flour
50 g (2 oz) brown rice flour or 100% semolina
2 teaspoons bicarbonate of soda
1 teaspoon cinnamon

Coating
50 g (2 oz) shelled, unsalted peanuts, finely
    chopped
25 g (1 oz) wheatgerm

MAKES 36

Heat the oven to 180°C (350°F/Mark 4).

Have ready two greased baking sheets.

Put the chopped peanuts in a mixing bowl with the margarine and sugar. Beat together until light and fluffy. Continue, beating in the egg, followed by the molasses. Stir in the remaining ingredients to form a slightly tacky dough. Refrigerate, covered, for an hour to give the dough a chance to firm up a little. Then roll the mixture into individual balls about the size of a walnut. Combine the ingredients for the coating mixture on a sheet of greaseproof or kitchen paper. Lightly press the coating mix onto the balls of dough and arrange on the greased baking sheets allowing about 2.5 cm (1 in) around each biscuit for spreading during baking. As a guideline I find I can get 10 biscuits on a baking sheet measuring 28 × 31 cm (11 × 12½ in). By the way, resist the temptation to flatten the dough. This will happen automatically during baking and it achieves a better-looking biscuit if it happens naturally. Bake for 15 to 20 minutes or until *almost* firm. Leave to cool on the baking sheets for 5 minutes before lifting onto a wire rack to become cold and crisp. Store in an airtight tin.

Honey and Apricot Shortbread

The flavour of honey does come through. Very speedy to make – the sort of recipe that makes a nonsense out of packet mixes!

150 g (5 oz) 100% plain wholewheat flour
25 g (1 oz) brown rice flour or 100% semolina
25 g (1 oz) light, soft brown sugar
75 g (3 oz) vegetable margarine
50 g (2 oz) dried apricots, chopped
1-1½ tablespoons clear honey
1 tablespoon Demerara sugar

MAKES 12 WEDGES

Heat the oven to 170°C (325°F/Mark 3).

Put the first four ingredients into a bowl. Rub in the margarine until the mixture resembles coarse breadcrumbs. Add the chopped apricots and stir in just sufficient honey to bring the mixture together to a firm unsticky dough. Form into a ball. Select a flat baking sheet or the base of a flan tin, large enough to accommodate a 25.5-cm (10-in) round; sprinkle with additional rice flour or semolina. Transfer the ball of dough to the tin and roll out to a round 24 cm (9½ in) in diameter. Pinch the edge between thumb and forefinger and prick the centre all over with a fork. Using a large knife, mark into 12 wedges. Sprinkle the surface with Demerara sugar and bake in the centre of the oven for 30 minutes or until the shortbread feels firm in the centre. Remove and cut into the marked wedges. Cool on a wire rack and store in an airtight tin.

Hermits

An American biscuit that they would describe as a 'spiced dropped cookie'. They are lightly spiced, a little soft and spongy, but with a bit of a fruit and nut chew. Highly recommended!

120 ml (4 fl oz) clear honey
120 ml (4 fl oz) tahini (sesame seed paste)
1 tablespoon molasses or black treacle
2 eggs, lightly beaten
110 g (4 oz) coarsely chopped walnuts
110 g (4 oz) chopped dates
110 g (4 oz) raisins or sultanas
grated rind of 1 orange

175 g (6 oz) 100% plain wholewheat flour
1 teaspoon cinnamon
½ teaspoon allspice
½ teaspoon mace
½ teaspoon bicarbonate of soda

MAKES ABOUT 30

Heat the oven to 170°C (325°F/Mark 3).

Lightly grease two baking sheets.

Stir the ingredients into a bowl in the order in which they are given above, to form a fairly stiff sticky dough. Using a teaspoon, scoop walnut-sized heaps onto the greased baking sheets, allowing about 4 cm (1½ in) spreading space between each biscuit. Bake in the centre of the oven for 15 to 20 minutes or until the biscuits feel firm when pressed in the centre and the edges are just beginning to darken. Use a palette knife to remove them to a wire rack to cool. Store in an airtight container.

Nut Surprises

A lovely nutty bite! Each small, crispy biscuit has a nut stowed away inside. What kind of nut is up to you, but Brazils, walnut or pecan halves work best.

Biscuits
110 g (4 oz) vegetable margarine
50 g (2 oz) light, soft brown sugar
1 teaspoon natural vanilla essence
150 g (5 oz) 85% plain brown flour
2 tablespoons fine oatmeal
approximately 20 nut halves (e.g. Brazils, walnuts or pecans)

Coating
2 tablespoons light, soft brown sugar
3 tablespoons wheatgerm

MAKES ABOUT 20

Heat the oven to 180°C (350°F/Mark 4).

Lightly grease two baking sheets.

Put the margarine, sugar and vanilla in a mixing bowl and beat until paler in colour. Stir in the flours until the mixture comes together to form a dough that leaves the side of the bowl clean. Taking about a teaspoon of dough at a time, pat out the dough to a round in the palm of one hand. Place a nut half in the centre and enclose in the dough. Form into a neatish lozenge shape and bake in the centre of the oven for about 15 minutes, or until firm and tinged with brown.

While the biscuits are baking combine the coating ingredients together (easiest in a plastic bag). As soon as the biscuits are baked, drop them into the bag, one by one and press the coating mix gently onto them before removing to cool on a wire rack. Store in an airtight container.

Fresh Ginger Biscuits with Honey and Wheatgerm

Lovely, crisp, ginger snaps with a gentle, mellow ginger flavour – and not too sweet.

110 g (4 oz) 85% self-raising brown flour
25 g (1 oz) wheatgerm
1 teaspoon bicarbonate of soda
40 g (1½ oz) dark, soft brown sugar
50 g (2 oz) vegetable margarine
1½ teaspoons freshly grated ginger
2 tablespoons clear honey

MAKES 18

Heat the oven to 190°C (375°F/Mark 5).

Grease two baking sheets.

Put the flour, wheatgerm, bicarbonate of soda and sugar into a bowl. Rub in the sugar until it is uniformly distributed throughout the mixture and there are no lumps. Do likewise with the margarine. Add the freshly grated ginger and honey to the mixture and stir to form a stiffish dough. Form the dough into small balls between the palms of the hands and place on the greased baking sheets allowing about 4 cm (1½ in) spreading room between biscuits. Bake for 15 to 20 minutes or until biscuits are just firm in the centre. Cool on a wire rack and store in an airtight container.

Maximum Crunch Biscuits

The title says all. A good, basic biscuit for the family which could be made by the younger members.

175 g (6 oz) vegetable margarine
175 g (6 oz) light, soft brown sugar
1 egg
175 g (6 oz) 100% plain wholewheat flour
¼ teaspoon baking powder
¼ teaspoon bicarbonate of soda
110 g (4 oz) rolled oats
110 g (4 oz) shelled peanuts, finely chopped
50 g (2 oz) bran flakes breakfast cereal   MAKES ABOUT 40

Heat the oven to 170°C (325°F/Mark 3).

Liberally grease two baking sheets. (This recipe will require baking several batches of biscuits.)

Put the margarine and sugar into a bowl and beat until paler in colour. Beat in the egg, then stir in the remaining ingredients. Roll into walnut-sized balls, put onto the greased baking sheets and flatten with a fork.

Bake in the centre of the oven for 20 to 25 minutes or until firm and browned. Use a palette knife to remove the biscuits from the baking sheet to the cooling rack. Warning: if you leave them for several minutes they have a tendency to cling like limpets to the tray!

Decidedly Lemony Fig Rolls

Always one of my favourites when I was a child; I set to work to do a wholewheat version for this book, and, my goodness me, the result is streets ahead of anything you can buy!

Pastry
75 g (3 oz) vegetable margarine
175 g (6 oz) dark, soft brown sugar
1 egg, lightly beaten
150 g (5 oz) 100% plain wholewheat flour
150 g (5 oz) 85% plain brown flour
1 teaspoon natural vanilla essence
¼ teaspoon bicarbonate of soda

Filling
450 g (1 lb) dried figs
rind of 1 lemon
juice of ½ lemon

MAKES 24

First make the pastry. Beat the margarine and sugar together until paler in colour and fairly fluffy. Beat in the egg, a little at a time, then stir in the dry ingredients to form a stiff dough that leaves the side of the bowl clean. Form into a ball, wrap closely in cling film and chill for at least 30 minutes.

Next make the fig filling. Snip the hard central stalks from the figs and place the dried fruit in a food processor with the pared zest of the lemon (use a potato peeler for this) and the lemon juice. Process until the fig paste forms a ball.

Grease two baking sheets.

It is easiest to roll out the dough between two sheets of greaseproof paper to obtain a rectangle measuring 20 × 40 cm (8 × 16 in). Cut in half lengthwise to give two strips 10 × 40 cm (4 × 16 in), then in half across to give four rectangles measuring 10 × 20 cm (4 × 8 in). Divide the fig paste into four and form each portion into a 20-cm (8-in) long sausage. Lay these down the centre of each rectangle, then bring the pastry up around the fig paste to enclose it. Smooth the pastry joins together well, turn each large roll over so the seam is underneath and cut in half. You will now have eight large rolls. Place them on the greased baking sheets and chill for 30 minutes.

Heat the oven to 190°C (375°F/Mark 5). Bake the fig rolls in the centre of the oven for 15 to 20 minutes or until browned and firm. When baked, remove and using a sharp knife cut each roll carefully into three. Leave to cool before storing in an airtight container.

Craggy Heaps (top left)
Carob Chip and Peanut Biscuits (on tray)
Decidedly Lemony Fig Rolls (centre)
Folded Fruit Slices (bottom right)
Fresh Ginger Biscuits with Honey and Wheatgerm (left half of dish)
Nut Surprises (right half of dish)

Craggy Heaps

A good recipe for children. They turn out slightly more crunchy if they are baked on a baking sheet, but children might find it easier to spoon the mixture into the confines of paper cake cases set in bun tins.

2 eggs
50 g (2 oz) light, soft brown sugar
225 g (8 oz) pitted, chopped dates
110 g (4 oz) chopped walnuts
1 teaspoon natural vanilla essence
110 g (4 oz) bran flakes breakfast cereal   MAKES 20

Heat the oven to 180°C (350°F/Mark 4).

Either, grease a baking sheet or, have ready a patty tin lined with paper cake cases.

Place the eggs in a mixing bowl and beat well. Gradually beat in the sugar. Stir in the remaining ingredients in the order given above. When thoroughly mixed spoon into heaps either onto the greased baking sheet or into the paper cases. Bake in the centre of the oven for 15 to 20 minutes or until tinged with brown and firm to the touch. Leave to harden for a couple of minutes before using a palette knife to remove them to a wire rack to cool. Not so crunchy the day after they are baked, but still enjoyable.

Folded Fruit Slices

The fruit pulp can be made from any of the firmer seasonal fruits such as rhubarb, gooseberries, cooking apples, plums. Cook them to a non-watery pulp and use the minimum *amount of sugar to sweeten; the finished slices will taste all the better for it.*

Pastry
110 g (4 oz) vegetable margarine
50 g (2 oz) light, soft brown sugar
1 egg, separated
½ teaspoon natural vanilla essence
175 g (6 oz) plus 1 tablespoon 85% plain brown flour
¼ teaspoon baking powder

Filling
350 g (12 oz) prepared fruit (see above)
1-2 tablespoons light, soft brown sugar

Topping
50 g (2 oz) unskinned chopped almonds

MAKES 12

In a bowl combine the margarine, sugar, egg yolk and vanilla. Beat until smooth and slightly paler in colour. Stir in the flour and baking powder until the mixture comes together to form a soft dough that leaves the side of the bowl clean. Form the dough into a ball, wrap in a plastic bag or cling film and chill in the fridge for an hour.

Meanwhile rinse a medium-sized saucepan with water, put in the prepared fruit, cover with a lid and cook over a low heat for 10 minutes, shaking the pan occasionally to prevent the fruit sticking. (If it cooks gently there should be no need to add water.) Once the fruit is soft, remove the lid, mash it down with a wooden spoon and continue to cook, stirring frequently until it is a thick pulp. Remove the pan from the heat and stir in the minimum sugar to taste. Leave until cold.

Heat the oven to 170°C (325°F/Mark 3).

Grease a large baking sheet.

Divide the chilled dough in half. Roll out half to a rectangle 18 × 28 cm (7 × 11 in) between two sheets of greaseproof paper. Spread half the cold fruit pulp in a strip down the central third of the dough. Now use the base sheet of greaseproof paper to help lift and fold each long side of pastry inwards over the filling, leaving a slight gap between the two edges where they meet in the centre. Whisk the egg white until just foamy and brush the pastry lightly. Now fold in half lengthwise to form a long, narrow, four-layered strip. Transfer to the baking sheet with the aid of the greaseproof paper. Repeat with the remaining dough. Lightly brush both strips with beaten egg white and sprinkle thickly with chopped almonds.

Bake in the centre of the oven for 45 minutes. Remove and leave to cool on the baking sheet for 10 minutes before slicing obliquely into 4-cm (1½-in)-wide slices (the cook eats the corner pieces). Using a palette knife, transfer to a wire rack to cool completely.

Carob Chip and Peanut Biscuits

Really crunchy and not too sweet. If you are using whole peanuts with their skins on, put them in a bowl and pound briefly with the end of a rolling pin. The skins will float off – don't bother to pick them out, add it all to the biscuit dough – more roughage!

110 g (4 oz) vegetable margarine
75 g (3 oz) light, soft brown sugar
1 egg
½ teaspoon natural vanilla essence
75 g (3 oz) 100% plain wholewheat flour
110 g (4 oz) 85% plain brown flour
½ teaspoon bicarbonate of soda
25 g (1 oz) wheatgerm
75 g (3 oz) carob (or chocolate) chips
75 g (3 oz) shelled peanuts   MAKES 30

Heat the oven to 180°C (350°F/Mark 4).

Grease some baking sheets. These biscuits will need baking in several batches.

In a mixing bowl beat the margarine and sugar together until light and fluffy. Beat in the eggs and vanilla, then gradually incorporate the remaining ingredients. The biscuit dough will be soft but not too soft to handle. Briefly roll into walnut-sized balls and transfer to a baking sheet. Using the flat of your hand press them out to rounds about ½ cm (¼ in) thick. Bake for 15 to 20 minutes in the centre of the oven until well browned. Remove from the oven and leave to cool and firm up on the baking sheet for a couple of minutes, then transfer the biscuits to cool on a wire rack. As soon as they are cold they need to be stored in an airtight container. If they are left out they tend to go soft rather quickly.

Amazingly Easy Carob and Almond Slices

Children might enjoy tackling these. They are a rather unusual biscuit, not too sweet, straightforward to make and unsticky to boot!

Biscuits

425 g (15 oz) 85% plain brown flour
1 teaspoon baking powder
175 g (6 oz) carob, or plain chocolate polka dots
110 g (4 oz) unskinned chopped almonds
3 eggs
175 g (6 oz) light, soft brown sugar
150 ml (¼ pint) vegetable oil
1 teaspoon natural almond essence

To sprinkle

40 g (1½ oz) sesame seeds or chopped pumpkin
  seeds

MAKES ABOUT 20

Heat the oven to 190°C (375°F/Mark 5).

Have ready a greased baking sheet 32.5 cm (13 in) long; the width does not matter.

Put the first four ingredients in a mixing bowl. Measure the remaining ingredients into a smaller bowl; beat these with a rotary whisk to mix them thoroughly. Pour the wet ingredients onto the dry and mix to a thick dough. Divide the dough in half and roll this on the work surface into a rough sausage shape, slightly shorter than 32.5 cm (13 in) in length. (Flour is not necessary; the oil in the dough effectively keeps hands and surface clean and unsticky.) Transfer the 'sausage' to the baking sheet and pat it flat to form a rectangle of dough about 10 cm (4 in) wide and 30 cm (12 in) long. Sprinkle the surface thickly with sesame or chopped pumpkin seeds. Bake for 20 to 25 minutes in the centre of the oven or until the dough feels firm to the touch. Remove from the oven and leave to cool. When cold slice at an angle into bars about 2.5 cm (1 in) wide. Arrange these on a grill pan and grill on both cut sides until browned. Leave to cool. Store in an airtight tin.

Muesli Chews (top left)
Citrus Slice (top right)
Amazingly Easy Carob and Almond Slices (centre right)
Malted Banana Bars (centre left)
Wheat, Sultana and Cashew Bars (bottom left)
Poppy Seed Biscuits (bottom right)

Poppy Seed Biscuits

Sesame seeds can be used just as well. A straightforward biscuit recipe – they can be cut into bars or squares and keep well in an airtight container.

175 g (6 oz) vegetable margarine
110 g (4 oz) light, soft brown sugar
1 teaspoon natural vanilla essence
110 g (4 oz) ground unblanched almonds
275 g (10 oz) 100% wholewheat flour
25 g (1 oz) semolina

¼ teaspoon each ginger, cinnamon and mace
a little beaten egg
60 g (2½ oz) poppy seeds

MAKES 24 OR 32

Heat the oven to 190°C (375°F/Mark 5).

Lightly grease a large Swiss roll tin measuring 32.5 × 23 cm (13 × 9 in).

In a mixing bowl beat together the margarine and sugar. Gradually stir in the vanilla essence, almonds, flour, semolina and spices. By now the mixture will resemble a mealy sort of mix. Spread this evenly in the greased tin, then press it down with the back of a spoon. Brush the surface with beaten egg and sprinkle with the seeds. Bake in the centre of the oven for 25 to 30 minutes. The mixture will feel firm in the centre when baked. Cool slightly before cutting into 32 bars or 24 squares.

Citrus Slices

Simply delicious, rather delicate slices with a good lemony tang. They are marginally better when eaten the day they are made but still very good up to a week later.

Base
110 g (4 oz) 85% plain brown flour
25 g (1 oz) wheatgerm
25 g (1 oz) Muscovado sugar
2 tablespoons bran
75 g (3 oz) vegetable margarine

Topping
175 g (6 oz) light, soft brown sugar
2 tablespoons 85% plain brown flour
¼ teaspoon baking powder
grated rind and juice of 2 smallish lemons
2 eggs, beaten

MAKES 32

Heat the oven to 180°C (350°F/Mark 4). Have ready a shallow, square tin, 21.5 × 21.5 × 3 cm (8½ × 8½ ×1¼ in). It is not necessary to grease or line it in any way.

Put all the ingredients for the base into a bowl and rub in the margarine until the mixture resembles breadcrumbs. Transfer this to the baking tin and press it level with the back of a spoon. Bake in the centre of the oven for 20 minutes.

Meanwhile, mix the ingredients for the topping in the bowl, one by one in the order they appear in the recipe. When the base has baked for 20 minutes pour the topping over and return it to the oven to bake for a further 30 minutes or until it is golden brown on the surface and just firm. Cool in the tin and cut into bars when cold. The size and shape of these are up to you so the number I have given is rather arbitrary, but may give some sort of guide.

Malted Banana Bars

Lovely, flavoursome and moist.

110 g (4 oz) vegetable margarine	*½ teaspoon bicarbonate of soda*
75 g (3 oz) dark, soft brown sugar	*2 bananas*
2 tablespoons malt extract	*1 tablespoon sesame seeds*
110 g (4 oz) 85% self-raising brown flour	
110 g (4 oz) rolled oats	MAKES 15 OR 16

Heat the oven to 180°C (350°F/Mark 4).

Have ready a shallow, square tin measuring 3 cm (1¼ in) deep and 18 cm (7 in) square, liberally greased. Do not attempt to bake this recipe in a shallower tin.

Combine the margarine, sugar and malt in a saucepan and warm gently until the margarine has melted.

Meanwhile mix the dry ingredients together in a bowl. Pour in the melted mix and stir to form a dough. Press half the dough into the prepared tin. Mash the bananas to a pulp and spread over the top. Taking small lumps of the remaining dough, flatten them slightly between the hands and join in a patchwork quilt over the mashed banana. Do not worry if there are gaps, these will join up during the baking. Sprinkle the surface with sesame seeds. Bake in the centre of the oven for 30 minutes. At this stage cover loosely with foil and bake for a further 20 to 30 minutes. The mixture will still seem rather soft but remove from the oven and leave to cool for 5 minutes before cutting into squares or bars. Turn out onto a wire rack to cool.

Muesli Chews

Very like those snack bars on sale in shops, but without the coconut, an ingredient I am not very fond of.

75 g (3 oz) 100% plain wholewheat flour	*1 tablespoon malt extract*
75 g (3 oz) rolled oats	*2 tablespoons vegetable oil*
25 g (1 oz) wheatgerm	*25 g (1 oz) vegetable margarine*
50 g (2 oz) dried apricots, finely chopped	*50 g (2 oz) dark, soft brown sugar*
50 g (2 oz) sultanas	
50 g (2 oz) sunflower seeds	
1 tablespoon honey	MAKES 12

Heat the oven to 170°C (325°F/Mark 3).

Grease a small Swiss roll tin 18 × 28 cm (7 × 11 in).

Combine the first six ingredients together in a bowl. Put all the remaining ingredients into a saucepan and warm gently until melted. Pour into the dry ingredients and mix well until the mixture comes together to form a coarse crumble. Press this into the tin and bake in the centre of the oven for 30 minutes or until golden brown and firm. Leave to cool for a few minutes before cutting into bars (use a sharp knife!). Cool on a wire rack and store in an airtight tin.

Wheat, Sultana and Cashew Bars

High fibre! Cashew nuts are used in the recipe, but as they are rather expensive, you may prefer to substitute almonds, walnuts or peanuts.

Base
110 g (4 oz) 100% plain wholewheat flour
75 g (3 oz) vegetable margarine
50 g (2 oz) dark, soft brown sugar
25 g (1 oz) bran

Topping
2 eggs
175 g (6 oz) dark, soft brown sugar
1 teaspoon natural vanilla essence
50 g (2 oz) 85% plain brown flour
½ teaspoon baking powder
4 Shredded Wheat biscuits, crumbled
150 g (5 oz) cashew nuts, chopped
50 g (2 oz) sultanas
2 teaspoons lemon juice   MAKES 24

Heat the oven to 180°C (350°F/Mark 4).

Grease a shallow 21.5- to 23-cm (8½- to 9-in) square tin. If the only tin you have is a deep, square cake tin use that, it will just mean that to turn the cooked bars out of the tin it is a little more difficult (but no serious problem).

First make the base, by putting all the ingredients in a bowl. Rub in the margarine until the mixture forms large, mealy crumbs. Press this evenly into the base of the tin using the back of a spoon. Bake in the centre of the oven for 20 minutes.

Meanwhile, prepare the topping. Break the eggs into a mixing bowl. Add the sugar and vanilla essence, then whisk until thickened and pale. Fold in the remaining ingredients and spoon onto the baked base. Spread with the back of a spoon to cover the base. Return to the oven to bake at the same temperature for 30 minutes. Leave to cool in the tin before cutting into 24.5 × 2.5-cm (2 × 1-in) bars.

ALL MANNER OF BREADS

Vitamin C Wholewheat Bread

This will take about 1½ hours from weighing out the flour to taking the bread from the oven. If you opt to use dried yeast bear in mind that this will take the extra 15 minutes needed to reconstitute it (i.e. to froth) before using. It is an excellent, well-behaved bread, very suitable for sandwiches, toast, etc.

675 g (1½ lb) 100% plain wholewheat flour
1 tablespoon dried yeast or 25 g (1 oz) fresh
  yeast
2 teaspoons salt
2 teaspoons Muscovado sugar
25-mg Vitamin C tablet
425 ml (¾ pint) warm water   MAKES 1 LARGE OR 2 SMALL LOAVES
1 tablespoon vegetable margarine   OR 12 BAPS

If using *dried yeast*, put 275 ml (½ pint) warm water into a small bowl. Add the Vitamin C tablet. Using a fork, whisk in the sugar, then the dried yeast and leave aside for 15 minutes to froth. Meanwhile combine the flour and salt in a mixing bowl, then rub in the margarine. Pour in the frothed yeast and a further 150 ml (¼ pint) warm water in which is dissolved the remaining teaspoon of sugar. Stir to form a dough.

If using *fresh yeast*, put the flour and salt in a mixing bowl and rub in the margarine. Place the fresh yeast, Vitamin C tablet and sugar in a small bowl. Gradually blend with some of the measured warm water. When all is dissolved, add to the flour mix with the remaining water and stir to form a dough.

In either case turn the dough out onto a clean work surface and knead for 10 minutes. No additional flour is necessary. Form into a ball and leave to one side, covered by the upturned bowl, whilst preparing the baking tins.

Select the appropriate tins, either one 900-g (2-lb) loaf tin *or* two 450-g (1 lb) loaf tins *or*, if making the baps or muffins, two baking sheets, grease and put to warm whilst shaping the bread. Drop it into the tins and enclose inside plastic bags, trapping a little air inside before sealing with a tie tag.

You will need to pre-heat the oven to 230°C (450°F/Mark 8) so I find the best place to rise the bread is on top of the stove. It will need about 30 minutes to rise. It is very tempting to let bread go on rising just a little bit longer, but try not to do this. The tops should be nicely rounded, showing no more than 2.5 cm (1 in) above the edge of the tin. Bake in the centre of the oven for 5 minutes, then reduce the heat to 220°C (425°F/Mark 7). Bake for a further 30 minutes. Turn out and tap the loaves on the base; they should sound hollow. Cool on a wire rack.

Notes
If you would prefer to bake, say, once a week, the recipes can readily be doubled to give enough dough to make two 900-g (2-lb) loaves or four 450-g (1-lb) loaves.
To freeze Wrap in heavy duty aluminium foil or plastic bags. The bread can be stored for up to six months.
To thaw Place the frozen foil-wrapped loaf in a hot oven 200°C (400°F/Mark 6) for 45 minutes or leave, wrapped at room temperature, for 3 to 6 hours depending on the size of the loaf. Rolls will take about 1½ hours to thaw at room temperature, or if wrapped in foil they can be put, frozen, in the oven at 230°C (450°F/Mark 8) for 15 minutes.

Overnight rise The basic rule is very simple: the lower the temperature the slower the yeast works. So, if it fits in better with your work schedule, mix the dough the night before with cool water, knead and put into the tin(s) and place in a sealed plastic bag. Leave in the refrigerator overnight. The following morning heat the oven and transfer the bread from fridge to oven to bake, as above.

Variations

Wholewheat Baps

Make the dough as above and knead for 10 minutes. Rest, covered, for 10 minutes, then divide into 12 pieces. Knead each piece to a round and transfer to a floured baking sheet. Liberally flour your hands and press the dough rounds down to form flattened discs. Push your thumb straight down through the centre to give each bap its traditional marking. Put the baking sheets inside large plastic bags, seal and leave the baps to rise for 20 to 25 minutes. Set the oven to heat to 240°C (475°F/Mark 9) whilst the baps are rising. Transfer the baps to the oven and reduce the temperature to 220°C (425°F/Mark 7). Bake for 10 minutes. Transfer to a wire rack, cover with a clean teatowel and leave to cool.

English Wholewheat Muffins

Make the dough as above and knead for 10 minutes. Rest, covered, for 10 minutes. Dust the work surface with a little fine semolina or cornmeal and roll the dough out to 1 cm (½ in) thick. Cut into 9-cm (3½-in) rounds with a plain cutter. Re-roll the trimmings and cut out additional rounds until all the dough is used up. Place the rounds on an ungreased baking sheet, dusted with semolina or cornmeal. Place the baking sheet inside a large plastic bag and seal. Leave in a warm place to rise for 15 to 30 minutes.

Heat a griddle or heavy-based frying pan over a medium heat, then grease lightly with vegetable oil. Put the muffins to cook immediately turning the heat down to low. They will need about 7 minutes on each side, and need to be baked in about five batches. Serve split, toasted and buttered. They can be stored for about two days in a sealed plastic bag.

MAKES 20 TO 22 MUFFINS

Pull-Apart Loaf

The following loaves are, again, based on the basic Vitamin C Wholewheat Bread dough. What I have done is divide the dough in half to make two different types. Both are based on a crown loaf, an attractive loaf made up of small rounds of dough baked together in a sandwich tin.

Here, half the dough is divided into balls, and each ball coated in a different seed or grain. They are put together in one 20-cm (8-in) sandwich tin to bake. It makes a very good-looking party piece, or a useful bread where each member of the family can opt for a favourite topping.

½ quantity Vitamin C Wholewheat Bread dough

Suggested toppings
oatmeal or rolled oats
cornmeal
poppy seeds
cracked wheat (kibbled wheat)
sesame seeds
bran flakes
barley flakes
sunflower seeds
malted wheat flour

Make the dough as described and knead for 10 minutes. Rest, covered, for 10 minutes. Meanwhile grease a sandwich tin, 20 cm (8 in) in diameter and assemble your chosen selection of toppings. Briefly knead the dough again before dividing into nine equal pieces. One by one, form each piece into a neat ball, dampen with water and coat each ball in one of the selected toppings. Arrange them in the sandwich tin, eight in a circle with one in the centre. Place in a plastic bag, seal and leave on top of the stove to rise for 30 minutes or until there are no gaps between the pieces of dough. While the dough is rising have the oven heating to 230°C (450°F/Mark 8). Bake the rolls for 20 to 25 minutes. Turn out and cool on a wire rack.

Ploughman's Lunch Loaf (top left)
Vitamin C Wholewheat Bread (top right)
Wholewheat Rolls (centre right)
Wholewheat Baps (centre left)
English Wholewheat Muffins (bottom left)
Pull-Apart Loaf (bottom right)

Ploughman's Lunch Loaf

With the remaining quantity of dough try the same loaf done a slightly different way. This time each ball of dough is rolled in a mixture of chopped onion and grated cheese.

½ quantity Vitamin C Wholewheat Bread
   dough
1 medium-sized onion, chopped
75 g (3 oz) grated Cheddar cheese
freshly ground black pepper

Have ready a greased 20-cm (8-in) sandwich tin.

Proceed in exactly the same manner as for the Pull-Apart Loaf, dividing the remaining dough into nine equal pieces. Toss together the grated cheese, onion and freshly ground black pepper on a plate. Roll each shaped ball of dough in this mixture and arrange in the tin in the same way. Rise and bake in the same way. Check that this loaf is not becoming too brown. If it is, cover with a sheet of foil for the rest of the baking. Run a knife around the edge before turning out on a wire rack to cool. Of course, if you prefer you can make two of the same type of loaf. Should you want to make two Ploughman's Lunch Loaves, try making the basic recipe using 275 ml (½ pint) beer, made up to 425 ml (¾ pint) with hot water.

Pitta Bread

This Mediterranean bread has become immensely popular in the last few years, probably because its pocket shape is such a useful container for all manner of fillings. It is difficult for the home cook to reproduce the chewy pliability of the commercial product. I had just arrived at the technique below when Suzy Benghiat's book Middle Eastern Cookery, *came onto the market. Those who would like to pursue the matter may like to try her slightly different Arabic bread which Mrs. Benghiat cooks under a grill.*

1 recipe Vitamin C Wholewheat Bread, rested
   for the initial 10 minutes only
a little additional flour   MAKES 6

The size of the pittas is a matter of preference, but try this method first. Divide the dough into six. On a clean work surface roll out each piece to an oval about 30.5 × 10 cm (12 × 4 in). Dust a little flour down the length of the oval, then brush the edges with water. Fold in half by bringing the bottom up to the top to give a pitta 15 cm (6 in) long. Press the edges together to seal. Arrange on lightly floured baking sheets and enclose in plastic bags. Seal and leave to rise for 15 minutes.

Heat the oven to 230°C (450°F/Mark 8).

Bake at the top of the oven for 10 to 15 minutes or until lightly browned. Slash across the fold and stack the bread wrapped in a clean, slightly damp teatowel until cool. This will give the bread its pliability. Ease each pocket apart and insert the desired filling. This bread has to be eaten fresh.

The Grant Loaf

So-called because it was invented by Doris Grant as part of her campaign to encourage the nation to eat a healthier diet. It does not require any kneading, it is simply mixed, the dough put into a tin and left to rise and then baked. The whole process takes about 1 hour 20 minutes from the weighing of the flour to taking the baked loaf from the oven, but knock 10 to 15 minutes off this time if you use fresh yeast. It gives a fairly dense, heavy loaf and is really best eaten the same day.

450 g (1 lb) 100% wholewheat flour
1½ teaspoons salt
25 g (1 oz) vegetable margarine
2 teaspoons brown sugar or honey or malt
*   extract or molasses*
355-380 ml (12-13 fl oz) warm water
10 g (½ oz) fresh yeast or 2 teaspoons dried
*   yeast*

Liberally grease one 900-g (2-lb) loaf tin or two 450-g (1-lb) loaf tins.

If using *fresh yeast* have the flour and salt ready in a bowl with the margarine rubbed in. Measure 355 ml (12 fl oz) water into a measuring jug, blend in the yeast and sugar or other sweetener and pour into the dry ingredients. Stir to form a dough; the consistency needs to be slightly wetter than that of a kneaded dough.

If using *dried yeast*, measure 150 ml (¼ pint) hand-hot water into a bowl. With a fork whisk in the sugar or other sweetener followed by the yeast and leave aside in a warm place for 15 minutes until frothy. Meanwhile combine the flour and salt in a bowl and rub in the margarine. Pour the yeast liquid into the flour with sufficient additional hand-hot water to form a slightly wettish dough.

When the dough is ready scoop it into the greased tin(s), seal inside a plastic bag and leave to rise on top of the stove for 30 to 40 minutes whilst the oven is pre-heating to 200°C (400°F/Mark 6). Once the dough has risen to within about ½ cm (¼ in) of the top of the tin(s) transfer to the oven to bake; 45 minutes for a 900-g (2-lb) loaf, 35 minutes for the 450-g (1-lb) size. Cool on a wire rack.

Pitta Bread

Rye and Caraway Seed Bread

Usually quite a difficult bread to make with the highly variable types of rye flour on the market and rye having so little gluten anyway. In this recipe I have played it safe by using quite a high proportion of wheatflour with the rye and there should be no trouble in achieving a good bread with the minimum of fuss.

450 g (1 lb) 100% wholewheat flour
225 g (8 oz) rye flour
2 teaspoons salt
1½ teaspoons caraway seeds
2 teaspoons Easy Blend yeast or 2 teaspoons
   dried yeast or ½ oz fresh yeast
25-mg Vitamin C tablet
1 tablespoon molasses or black treacle
380-425 ml (13-15 fl oz) warm water
2 tablespoons vegetable oil

Glaze
2 teaspoons cornflour
150 ml (¼ pint) boiling water
2 teaspoons caraway seeds

MAKES 2 LOAVES

Put the first four ingredients into a bowl.

If using *Easy Blend yeast* stir this into the flour mix. Add the molasses and Vitamin C tablet to 275 ml (½ pint) warm water and pour into the dough with the oil and sufficient additional water to combine to a soft but not sticky dough. It is now ready to knead.

If using *dried yeast* measure 275 ml (½ pint) hand-hot water into a separate bowl. Using a fork, whisk in the Vitamin C tablet, molasses, then the dried yeast. Leave aside in a warm place for 15 minutes to froth.

If using *fresh yeast* blend into a little of the measured water with the molasses and Vitamin C tablet. Make sure all has dissolved smoothly.

Add the dried or fresh yeast mixture to the flour with the oil and sufficient water to form a soft but not sticky dough. Turn all mixes out onto a work surface and knead for 10 minutes. Cover the dough with the upturned bowl whilst greasing a large baking sheet.

Heat the oven to 220°C (425°F/Mark 7). Knead the dough again, briefly, then divide it in half. Shape into two oval loaves and place on the baking sheet allowing enough space between for expansion during rising and baking. Put the baking sheet inside a large plastic bag, leaving a little air inside, and seal with a tie tag. Put to rise on top of the stove for 30 to 40 minutes or until the dough springs back when pressed with a fingertip.

Meanwhile prepare the glaze. In a small bowl make a paste of the cornflour with a little cold water. Blend with the boiling water. If this does not thicken and clear, transfer to a saucepan and heat, stirring, until it does. Remove from the heat and put aside until ready to use.

Brush the risen dough with the glaze and sprinkle with additional caraway seeds. Make three diagonal slashes in each loaf. Bake for 15 minutes, then reduce the oven heat to 190°C (375°F/Mark 5) for a further 35 to 40 minutes. Fifteen minutes from the end of cooking time brush once more with the cornflour glaze. When baked the loaves should sound hollow when tapped on the base. Cool on a wire rack.

Clockwise from top left:
Rye and Caraway Seed Bread, Wholewheat, Yogurt and Potato Bread
The Grant Loaf, Harvest Loaf, Multi-Grain Bread

Wholewheat, Yogurt and Potato Bread

A lovely moist, coarse-textured, well-flavoured, peasant-style bread. Also very good if cooked rice is substituted for the potato.

1 teaspoon brown sugar
2 teaspoons dried yeast
225 g (8 oz) potatoes, peeled and grated
275 ml (½ pint) yogurt
350 g (13 oz) 100% plain wholewheat flour
350 g (13 oz) strong, white unbleached flour
olive oil
cornmeal or 100% semolina, for baking   MAKES 1 LARGE LOAF

Measure the water into a bowl. Sprinkle in the sugar, followed by the yeast, whisk with a fork to dissolve and put aside in a warm place for 15 minutes to rise.

Meanwhile put the grated potatoes in a saucepan with the yogurt and warm gently to hand-hot; leave aside.

Put the wholewheat flour in a large bowl with 275 g (10 oz) of the strong unbleached flour. Put the remaining flour on the work surface in a heap. Pour the frothed yeast onto the bulk of the flour, followed by the warmed potato and yogurt mixture. Stir to a dough. Turn out onto the work surface floured with a little of the strong flour. Knead for 10 minutes using some of the strong flour to prevent sticking in the initial stages. It should not need more flour than the weighed amount and try to use the minimum anyway, it makes for a better loaf. Oil a large bowl, turn the kneaded dough in the bowl to coat it with oil, then cover with cling film and leave in a warm place to rise until doubled in size. Knead for 3 to 4 minutes, shape into a round and transfer to a baking sheet liberally dusted with cornmeal or semolina. Enclose this in a plastic bag, seal and leave to rise until again doubled in size.

Heat the oven to 190°C (375°F/Mark 5).

Bake the loaf in the upper third of the oven for 35 to 45 minutes. When baked it should sound hollow when tapped on the base. Cool on a wire rack.

Multi-Grain Bread

It is difficult to describe this bread. I suppose the first thing is to emphasize that it does not rise much. The end result is something between a sweet teabread and the conventional loaf – slightly sweet, with a nutty flavour and a fairly dense, moist consistency. I find it the sort of bread that I can slice and eat unbuttered at any time of the day!

845 ml (1½ pints) boiling water
75 g (3 oz) cracked wheat (bulgar or burghul)
75 g (3 oz) millet
4 tablespoons honey
1 rounded tablespoon dried yeast
3 tablespoons cooking oil
50 g (2 oz) rolled oats
75 g (3 oz) cornmeal
3 tablespoons wheatgerm
50 g (2 oz) non-fat dried milk powder
2 teaspoons salt
225 g (8 oz) strong white unbleached flour
550 g (1¼ lb) 100% plain wholewheat flour
110 g (4 oz) chopped walnuts, pumpkin seeds
    and/or sunflower seeds
bran flakes

MAKES 2 LOAVES

You will need two loaf tins, base measurement 20 × 10 cm (8 × 4 in) by 7 cm (2¾ in) high.

In a saucepan combine the boiling water, cracked wheat and millet. Bring to the boil, then simmer, covered, for 5 minutes. Remove from the heat, stir in the honey and cool to hand-hot (about 110°F). At this temperature the dried yeast can be stirred in and left for 15 minutes to develop. Pour this mixture into a bowl and stir in the oil, oats, cornmeal, wheatgerm, milk powder and salt. Now add the strong flour, then sufficient wholewheat flour to bring the mix together and form a manageable dough. Turn out onto a work surface and knead for about 10 minutes. It will be quite hard work because it will remain a somewhat sticky dough. Oil a large bowl, turn the dough in it to coat it with a film of oil, then cover with cling film and leave aside in a warm place for a couple of hours. There will not be much discernible rise, so don't get anxious about this. Knead for about a minute, then work the nuts into the dough until they are evenly distributed throughout. Divide the dough in half. Shape the dough, rolling it in bran flakes, and put into the greased loaf tins. Enclose in plastic bags and leave aside for about 2 hours in a warm place. Again don't look for much rise.

Heat the oven to 190°C (375°F/Mark 5). Bake side by side in the centre of the oven for about 45 minutes. Check after 30 minutes to make sure the loaves are not getting too brown. If there seems any danger of this, cover the tins with a sheet of foil. Run a knife around the sides of the loaves, then turn out onto a wire rack to cool.

Note Like most yeasted recipes this bread will freeze well. If you would prefer a less dense loaf with a greater rise, simply increase the amount of strong flour and use less wholewheat flour.

Harvest Loaf

This recipe makes 2 small loaves but as they freeze admirably I do not feel this is a drawback. It makes a lovely teatime loaf which will keep well, wrapped in foil. On occasions when I have not had powdered milk in the house I have very successfully substituted Horlicks! Seeds and fruits can likewise be adapted to what is available without the recipe suffering in any way.

1 tablespoon dried yeast	*50 g (2 oz) sultanas*
3 tablespoons honey plus 1 teaspoon	*50 g (2 oz) sunflower seeds*
1 egg	*1 egg yolk, to glaze*
2 tablespoons vegetable oil	
75 g (3 oz) cracked wheat (kibbled wheat)	
275 g (10 oz) 100% plain wholewheat flour	
110 g (4 oz) strong white unbleached flour	
4 tablespoons skimmed milk powder	
3 tablespoons wheatgerm	
1½ teaspoons salt	
75 g (3 oz) large raisins	MAKES 2 SMALL LOAVES

You will need two loaf tins, base measurement 16.5 × 7.5 cm (6½ × 3 in), of 845-ml (1½-pints) capacity. Grease the tins well.

In a small bowl combine 4 tablespoons hand-hot water with the teaspoon of honey. Sprinkle in the yeast, whisk with a fork and set aside for 15 minutes until frothy.

In a separate, larger bowl, whisk together the egg, 3 tablespoons honey and oil. Stir in the cracked wheat and set aside.

Finally, in a large mixing bowl (the bowl of a stand mixer if your machine is equipped with a dough hook) combine the flours, powdered milk, wheatgerm and salt. As soon as the yeast has a good 'head' on it pour it into the combined flours, followed by the egg mixture. Measure out 150 ml (¼ pint) hand-hot water. Add 120 ml (4 fl oz) of this to the mixture and start to stir to bring the mixture together to a dough. (If you have a machine equipped to deal with yeast doughs, start it here.) The aim is to achieve as wet a dough as possible whilst still being able to knead it in the initial stages without too much of a struggle. Add some of the remaining water if necessary.

Knead by hand for 10 minutes, by which time the dough will be springy and leave the work surface clean. Use as little flour as possible during kneading. Pile the raisins, sultanas and sunflower seeds onto the work surface and knead these into the dough. Grease a large mixing bowl, turn the dough in it to grease it also, cover with cling film and leave aside in a warm place until doubled in size – about 2 hours.

Turn the dough out onto a clean work surface, knead briefly, weigh and divide the dough in half. Shape into neat rolls the length of the tins, slip the dough into the tins and place in a plastic bag. Leave to rise in a warm place for about an hour or until the dough has formed a nicely rounded top above the edges of the tins. Combine the egg yolk with a teaspoon of water and brush the tops of the loaves with this glaze. Bake in the centre of the oven (pre-heated to 190°C/375°F/Mark 5) for 35 to 40 minutes. The loaves should then have a conker-brown crust and sound hollow when tapped on the base. Cool in the tins then store wrapped in foil.

Herbed Wholewheat Soda Bread

Over the years I have tried many variations of this recipe until I have ended up with this one which I cannot better. This quick type of bread is a great standby and very impressive served warm from the oven. Bear in mind that the flavouring can be varied to complement the food served. Seeds make good flavourings too: caraway, fennel, dill, cummin, celery, etc.

bran flakes for sprinkling
450 g (1 lb) 100% wholewheat flour
¾ teaspoon bicarbonate of soda
2 teaspoons cream of tartar
1 teaspoon honey or brown sugar
1 tablespoon chopped fresh marjoram
1 tablespoon chopped fresh basil
1 teaspoon chopped fresh thyme
25 g (1 oz) vegetable margarine
about 275 ml (½ pint) buttermilk, sour milk or
*   yogurt*

MAKES 1 LOAF

Heat the oven to 190°C (375°F/Mark 5). Sprinkle a baking sheet with bran flakes.

Put the dry ingredients into a bowl with the chopped herbs. Rub in the margarine. Add the buttermilk, sour milk or yogurt to the mixture, stirring to mix the ingredients to a soft dough. (Add a drop more milk if necessary.) Sprinkle the work surface with bran flakes, turn the dough out, knead slightly and shape into a round. Transfer to the baking sheet and cut the dough into four equal portions. Bake in the centre of the oven for 30 minutes. When baked a skewer inserted in the centre should come out clean. Cool on a wire rack. Eat warm and fresh.

Thumb-Stuck Bread

Delicious! If garlic and olive oil are your passion, this is a recipe for you.

275 ml (½ pint) hand-hot water
1 teaspoon brown sugar
1 tablespoon dried yeast
225 g (8 oz) 100% plain wholewheat flour
225 g (8 oz) strong, white unbleached flour
25 g (1 oz) wheatgerm
1 tablespoon rosemary leaves plus 1½
   teaspoons
1½ teaspoons salt
7 tablespoons olive oil
6 fat cloves garlic
cornmeal for baking   MAKES 1 LOAF

Pour 150 ml (¼ pint) of the water into a small bowl and whisk in the sugar followed by the dried yeast. Leave aside for 15 minutes until frothy.

In a large mixing bowl combine the flours, wheatgerm, 1½ teaspoons of the rosemary leaves and the salt. Pour the yeast into the dry ingredients with the remaining hand-hot water. Spoon in 4 tablespoons of olive oil and mix to a soft dough. Use a stand mixer equipped with a dough hook if possible for this initial stage of kneading. Once the dough forms a ball around the dough hook transfer to knead on a work surface. Alternatively scoop the dough out onto a lightly floured work surface and proceed to knead it using the minimum of flour until gradually, over a period of 10 minutes, it obtains a firm springy consistency that leaves your hands and the work surface clean. Oil the bowl and replace the dough in it. Cover with cling film and leave aside in a warm place for about 2 hours, or until doubled in size.

Meanwhile, heat the remaining 3 tablespoons of olive oil in a small saucepan with an ovenproof handle or a small flameproof handle. Remove the pan from the heat and add the peeled garlic cloves. Cover with a lid and transfer to the oven to bake at 180°C (350°F/Mark 4) for 20 minutes. The garlic should now be soft. Remove it to a separate bowl, add the remaining rosemary and mash together with a fork; reserve the olive oil.

Turn the risen dough out on the work surface and knead again for a minute or two. Shape into a smooth round. Scatter a heavy baking sheet with cornmeal and sit the ball of dough in the centre. Brush it with the garlic-flavoured olive oil and slip the baking sheet inside a plastic bag. Leave for 15 minutes so the dough has time to settle down and begin to expand a little. Then, taking a little of the garlic paste between thumb and forefinger push this right down into the dough forming about 10 indentations in the top of the loaf. Replace in the plastic bag and leave for a further 15 minutes until again doubled in size. Brush with oil again and bake in the centre of the oven for 40 to 50 minutes. When baked the loaf will sound hollow when tapped on its base.

Clockwise from top left:
Thumb-stuck Bread, Cypriot-Style Bread, Herbed Wholewheat Soda Bread
Pitta Bread, Crisp French Sticks

Cypriot-Style Bread

I ate the most delicious bread whilst on holiday in Cyprus and I have tried to recreate it here. Although flours, ovens and water are impossible to duplicate I have managed to get fairly close. Chop everything coarsely, leaving the olives almost whole.

1 recipe Wholewheat, Yogurt and Potato Bread
  (see page 138)
1 tablespoon olive oil
2 celery stalks, coarsely chopped
1 onion, coarsely chopped
4 tablespoons fresh mint, chopped
175 g (6 oz) pitted green and black olives
cornmeal or semolina, for baking   MAKES 1 LARGE LOAF

Heat the oven to 190°C (375°F/Mark 5).

Whilst the bread is having its initial rising, heat the olive oil in a saucepan. Fry the chopped celery and onion gently until *just* softened. Remove from the heat and stir in the remaining ingredients. Leave to cool. When the bread dough has doubled in size, knead it for a further 3 or 4 minutes, then gradually knead in all the vegetable mixture. Transfer the dough to a baking sheet thickly dusted with cornmeal or semolina, then rise and bake the dough as directed above. It will take slightly longer to bake, about 45 minutes. Cool on a wire rack. Best served unbuttered I think, with fish, cheeses and salads.

Crisp French Sticks

144

Crisp French Sticks

Made with a combination of wholewheat and malted wheat flour, with a little 100% semolina, this does make a French-style loaf with a lot of crunch. Ideal for lunches with cheese or pâté.

225 g (8 oz) malted wheat flour
175 g (6 oz) 100% wholewheat flour
50 g (2 oz) 100% semolina
1 teaspoon salt
25 g (1 oz) fresh yeast or 2 teaspoons dried yeast
about 275 ml (½ pint) warm water
1 tablespoon vegetable oil
1 tablespoon malt extract
25-mg Vitamin C tablet
a little cracked wheat for topping   MAKES 1 THICK OR 2 THIN STICKS

Combine the flours and salt in a bowl.

If using *fresh yeast*, crumble into the measured warm water, add the oil, malt and Vitamin C tablet, then whisk with a fork until all is dissolved. Stir into the flour mixture to form a dough.

If using *dried yeast*, measure out the hand-hot water, then whisk in the malt, Vitamin C tablet and dried yeast. Leave aside in a warm place for 15 minutes until frothy. Add to the combined flours with the oil and mix to a dough.

Turn the dough out onto a work surface and knead for 10 minutes. Cover with the upturned bowl and leave for 10 minutes.

Heat the oven to 220°C (425°F/Mark 7).

Lightly flour your largest baking sheet. Form the dough into either one, fatter, long loaf, or two long thin sticks. Transfer to the baking sheet, brush with water and sprinkle with cracked wheat. Using a very sharp knife make diagonal slashes down the length of each stick. Place the baking sheet in a plastic bag and leave on top of the stove to rise for 30 minutes.

Bake for 25 to 25 minutes. Cool briefly on a wire rack before serving.

This quantity can also be shaped to a round and baked on a baking sheet or baked in a 900-g (2-lb) loaf tin in which case increase the cooking time by 10 to 15 minutes.

Pizzas

Pizzas are a highly versatile food, nutritious and cheap into the bargain. Many people do not have time to make a full-blown kneaded and proved bread base. A perfectly acceptable base can be made by mixing a yeast dough and, straight away, using it to line a baking sheet, or whatever. This can then be covered and left to rise whilst the filling is prepared, which means about an hour of preparation time is saved. I have given a variety of different toppings for the quick bread base, but there are other styles of pizza within this section which I hope you will try when time and energy permit.

Wholewheat Quick Bread Base

This will spin out to a maximum and fit a large Swiss roll tin 33 × 23 cm (13 × 9 in) or give a thicker base in a small Swiss roll tin 28 × 18 cm (11 × 7 in). It is possible to push it out to a round anything from 25.5 to 35 cm (10 to 14 in) if you have a metal base big enough on which to bake it! (Quiche tin bases are useful for this if you have the bigger sizes.)

1 teaspoon dried yeast
1 teaspoon brown sugar
150 ml (¼ pint) hand-hot water
225 g (8 oz) 100% plain wholewheat flour

25 g (1 oz) wheatgerm
1 teaspoon salt
2 tablespoons vegetable oil

First combine the dried yeast and sugar in a small bowl, pour in the hand-hot water and whisk with a fork. Leave aside for 15 minutes to develop until frothy.

Meanwhile, combine the flour, wheatgerm and salt in a large bowl. Pour in the yeast mixture and measure in the oil. Mix to form a dough, then scoop out onto a floured work surface. Knead briefly then use as required.

If using a tin, roll the dough out to roughly the same size, then transfer the dough to the oiled tin and use your fingers to even out and press the dough up the sides and into corners. Brush the surface with a little oil and place the entire tin in a large, clean plastic bag. Leave aside in a warm place for 30 minutes.

Wholewheat Pizza with Leek, Feta Cheese and Walnut Topping

Base
1 recipe Wholewheat Quick Bread Base
  (page 146)
1 teaspoon mixed dried herbs
about 1 teaspoon vegetable oil

Topping
450 g (1 lb) leeks, trimmed
2 tablespoons vegetable oil
75 g (3 oz) coarsely chopped walnuts
juice of ½ lemon
110 g (4 oz) Feta cheese, crumbled
freshly ground black pepper
black olives, halved and pitted, to garnish

Make the Quick Bread Base, adding the mixed dried herbs to the dry ingredients. Use any of the tin sizes suggested in the basic recipe.

Heat the oven to 220°C (425°F/Mark 7).

Whilst the dough is proving prepare the filling. Slice each leek into four lengthways, then cut across into 1-cm (½-in)-wide strips. Plunge the chopped leek into a bowl of cold water to clean it, then scoop out with a colander. Leave to drain thoroughly whilst warming the oil in a saucepan. Turn the leeks in the oil, then cover and cook gently for 2 to 3 minutes. Uncover and turn up the heat until most of the excess liquid has evaporated. Remove the pan from the heat and leave to cool. Stir in the walnuts, lemon juice and crumbled cheese. Taste and season with freshly ground black pepper – it probably will not need any salt, the cheese will make it salty enough.

Spread the leek mixture evenly over the bread base and garnish the surface with the halved black olives. Bake in the centre of the oven for 15 to 20 minutes. Check to make sure the bread base is cooked underneath in the centre. Best eaten hot.

Quick Pan Pizza

If you can afford it, I would recommend olive oil for this recipe; the flavour does make a difference. Also, if you have any fresh herbs add a little to the filling, e.g., thyme, basil, marjoram.

Base	*Topping*
225 g (8 oz) 85% plain brown flour	*110 g (4 oz) mushrooms, wiped*
2 teaspoons baking powder	*3 spring onions, trimmed*
1 teaspoon dried oregano	*a handful of parsley sprigs*
salt and freshly ground black pepper	*1 clove garlic, peeled*
2 tablespoons vegetable oil	*3 tablespoons tomato purée*
4 tablespoons cold water	*2 teaspoons anchovy paste*
oil for frying	*2 tablespoons grated Parmesan cheese*
	a little oil

SERVES 2 OR 4

To make the base, combine the dry ingredients together in a bowl. Measure the oil into a small bowl and add 4 tablespoons water. Whisk together with a fork and pour into the dry ingredients. Stir to bring together to a soft but not sticky dough, adding a further 1-2 tablespoons water if required. Turn out onto a lightly floured work surface and knead briefly and lightly before rolling out to a round big enough to fit the base of a 23- to 25.5-cm (9- to 9½-in) frying pan.

Heat the frying pan before pouring in sufficient oil to give a depth of about ½ cm (¼ in). When hot, slip the dough into the pan and cook over a moderate heat for about 5 minutes, checking that the underside is not browning too much. Meanwhile, liberally oil a dinner plate. Invert the pizza base onto the plate, return the pan to the heat and gently slip the dough back into it to cook the other side for a further 5 minutes. As it cooks spread the surface with the tomato purée followed by the anchovy. The mushrooms, onions, parsley and garlic can then be either piled on a chopping board together and finely chopped, or whizzed in a food processor for about 10 seconds. Sprinkle this mixture over the pizza and drizzle a little oil over the top. Lastly sprinkle with Parmesan cheese. When 5 minutes has elapsed and the underside is brown, finish the cooking by placing the pan under a hot grill for a further 4 to 5 minutes. Serve hot. It is also very good cold.

Four Seasons Wholewheat Pizza

This topping has an aubergine purée base, then a different ingredient is put on each quarter of the pizza. Here I have used mushrooms, courgettes, a pepper and tomatoes. Any other seasonal variation can be used as long as it complements all the others – useful if one member of the family dislikes a particular vegetable that another loves!

Base

1 recipe Wholewheat Quick Bread Base
  (page 146)
1 teaspoon mixed herbs
about 1 teaspoon vegetable oil

Aubergine purée

450 g (1 lb) aubergines (the longer, thinner
  variety, rather than the roundish ones)
salt
1 clove garlic, crushed
juice of 1 lemon
a handful of parsley sprigs
1 spring onion, with green top

Vegetable topping

110 g (4 oz) button mushrooms
2 small courgettes
1 red or green pepper
2 tomatoes
3 tablespoons grated Parmesan cheese

SERVES 4-6

Make the Quick Bread Base, adding the mixed dried herbs to the dry ingredients. Use to line a large Swiss roll tin 33 × 23 cm (13 × 9 in).

Whilst the dough is proving cook the aubergines. Use a roasting tin or grill pan on top of the stove. Cook the aubergines in this over a moderate heat turning them regularly as they cook, until they become blackened and soft. This will probably take about 20 minutes. (If you have never done this before, it can be slightly nerve-racking, but it does produce a better-flavoured purée with no cooking oils needed.) Slice the aubergines in half lengthwise, put in a colander, sprinkle with salt and leave to drain for 15 minutes whilst you slice the vegetables. Wipe and slice the mushrooms and courgettes. De-seed the pepper and slice very thinly. Slice the tomatoes but not quite so thinly. Sauté all but the tomatoes, separately and briefly in a little hot oil.

Rinse and pat the aubergines dry on kitchen paper. Peel off the blackened skin and purée the pulp in a processor or liquidizer with the garlic, lemon juice, parsley and spring onion. Alternatively the aubergine pulp can be mashed and the finely chopped ingredients added separately. Spread the aubergine purée over the pizza base and cover a quarter of the top with the slices of each vegetable. Sprinkle with Parmesan and bake in the top third of the oven for 15 to 20 minutes. Serve hot.

Clockwise from top left:
Four Seasons Wholewheat Pizza
Onion and Olive Pizza
Wholewheat Pizza with Tapenade and Roasted Peppers
Wholewheat Pizza with Leek, Feta Cheese and Walnut Topping
Quick Pan Pizza
Centre: Pizza Alla Fiorentina

Onion and Olive Pizza

This pizza recipe is made along the more traditional lines. It makes a substantial meal needing only a salad to be served with it. I have given shallots as an alternative to onions – whilst the peeling is laborious they do make for a good pizza!

Base

10 g (½ oz) dried yeast
240 ml (8 fl oz) lukewarm skimmed milk (or
   water)
1 teaspoon brown sugar
300 g (11 oz) 100% plain wholewheat flour
225 g (8 oz) strong white unbleached flour
50 g (2 oz) vegetable margarine
1 teaspoon salt
2 eggs

SERVES 6-8

Topping

825 g (1¾ lb) Spanish onions or shallots
3 tablespoons olive oil
150 ml (¼ pint) dry white wine
150 ml (¼ pint) fresh half-cream (12%
   butterfat)
2 teaspoons Dijon mustard
¼ teaspoon freshly grated nutmeg
110 g (4 oz) green olives, pitted and coarsely
   chopped

Garnish

small can anchovy fillets in oil
6 green olives, pitted and halved
50 g (2 oz) freshly grated Parmesan cheese

Put the dried yeast in a small bowl. Whisk in half the warmed milk or water and sugar. Leave aside for 15 minutes until frothy. Meanwhile place 225 g (8 oz) of the 100% wholewheat flour and the unbleached flour together in a mixing bowl with the margarine and salt. Rub in the margarine until smoothly incorporated into the flours. When the yeast is frothy, break the egg into the same bowl, adding the remaining warmed milk and water and whisk together with a fork. Pour onto the flours and combine to a soft dough. Use the remaining 75 g (3 oz) 100% wholewheat flour to dust the surface. Knead the dough for 10 minutes. In the initial stages more flour will have to be added to prevent the dough sticking but keep it to a minimum. Certainly no more than the 75 g (3 oz) should be required to obtain a smooth, unsticky dough. After kneading, oil your hands and smooth them over the ball of dough. Leave the dough on the work surface, covered by the upturned bowl, for 1 hour or until doubled in size.

Meanwhile prepare the filling. Peel and coarsely chop the onions or shallots. Heat the olive oil in a large pan and gently fry the onion for 10 minutes until softened but not coloured. Turn up the heat, pour in the wine and cook briskly until it is almost all evaporated. Add the cream, mustard and grated nutmeg and continue to cook gently, stirring until the onion mixture is creamy but not too runny. Stir in the olives and remove the pan from the heat to cool. Taste and season lightly if necessary.

Heat the oven to 220°C (425°F/Mark 7).

Select a large baking sheet, about 32.5 × 30 cm (13 × 12 in) to 43 × 30 cm (17 × 12 in). The size is not critical, but any smaller than the size specified would give an unpleasantly thick bread base. Do not grease the baking sheet but pat the dough out gradually to cover the surface and form a slight rim around the edge to contain the filling. Spread the filling over the top. Sprinkle with the Parmesan cheese and arrange the anchovy fillets and olives in a decorative pattern on the surface. Do not waste the oil from the can of anchovies; drizzle this over the surface of the pizza, then bake in the top half of the oven for 20 minutes. Check that the pizza is cooked by sliding a palette knife or fish slice under it and lifting it to make sure the underside is crisp and lightly browned. Serve hot.

Wholewheat Pizza with Tapenade and Roasted Peppers

A tapenade is a sauce from the Provence region of France and, according to Elizabeth David, the essential ingredient is capers. The other ingredients are olives (usually black but I use green in the recipe), anchovies, garlic and olive oil. Here I have spread it over the pizza base and covered it with roasted sliced peppers – delicious!

Bread base
1 recipe Wholewheat Quick Bread Base
   (page 146)
1 teaspoon mixed dried herbs
about 1 teaspoon vegetable oil

Topping
150 g (5 oz) pitted green olives
1 50-g (1¾-oz) can anchovy fillets in oil
50 g (2 oz) drained capers
1 clove garlic
1 teaspoon wholegrain mustard
freshly ground black pepper
about 4 tablespoons vegetable oil
2 green peppers
2 red peppers
25 g (1 oz) grated Parmesan cheese

Make the Quick Bread Base, adding the mixed dried herbs to the dry ingredients, and use the dough in any of the shapes suggested in the basic recipe.

Heat the oven to 220°C (425°F/Mark 7).

Whilst the dough is proving make the filling. Place the olives, drained anchovy fillets (reserving the oil) and capers, garlic and mustard in a food processor or liquidizer. Start the machine and slowly drip in first the reserved anchovy oil, then about 2 tablespoons of the vegetable oil, just as much as it takes to give a soft sauce. Turn off the machine; taste the sauce and add lemon juice and freshly ground black pepper as required.

To roast the peppers, halve, de-seed, then cut into eighths. Arrange, skin side up, on a grill pan and grill until thoroughly black. Allow to cool slightly, then strip off the blackened skins. Slice the pepper sections into thin strips.

Spread the tapenade on the bread base and top with an even layer of the mixed green and red pepper strips. Sprinkle with the Parmesan cheese and drizzle a further 2 tablespoons of oil over the surface. Bake for 15 to 20 minutes in the centre of the oven. Make sure that the bread base is cooked underneath in the centre before removing. Serve hot, or cold for a picnic or packed lunch.

Pizza Alla Fiorentina

I am assured by a Florentine that such a pizza does not actually exist in Florence, but the title does give some idea of the ingredients – eggs baked on top of a flavoursome spinach mixture. Ideally the egg yolks should still be runny when the pizza is served.

Base

1 recipe Wholewheat Quick Bread Base
   (see page 146)
1 teaspoon dill weed
about 1 teaspoon vegetable oil

Topping

450 g (1 lb) fresh spinach, trimmed and
   washed
½ teaspoon salt
2 tablespoons vegetable oil
1 bunch spring onions, trimmed and chopped
110 g (4 oz) Feta cheese, crumbled
225 g (8 oz) cottage cheese
1 large clove garlic, crushed
generous squeeze of lemon juice
freshly ground black pepper
6 small eggs   SERVES 6

Make the Quick Bread Base, adding the dill weed to the dry ingredients. You will need a large Swiss roll tin 32.5 × 23 cm (13 × 9 in) although if the size varies by 2.5 cm (1 in) either way it does not matter. Roll the dough out to roughly the same size as the tin. Transfer the dough to the sheet and use your fingers to even out and press the dough up the sides and into corners. Brush the surface with a little oil and place the entire tin in a large, clean plastic bag. Leave aside in a warm place for 30 minutes.

   Heat the oven to 220°C (425°F/Mark 7).

   Whilst the dough is proving make the filling. Pack the wet spinach into a large saucepan, sprinkle with salt, then cover and cook over a moderate heat for just as long as it takes for the leaves to wilt. Remove the pan from the heat and drain the spinach in a colander. When sufficiently cool, squeeze the leaves to get rid of most of the excess water. Transfer the spinach to a chopping board and chop coarsely. Add the oil to the saucepan and return to the heat. Very briefly fry the spring onions, remove from the heat and stir in the chopped spinach and all the remaining ingredients except the eggs. Taste and season if necessary. Spread this mixture evenly over the bread base. Using the back of a spoon make six firm indentations in the spinach. Break the eggs carefully into these pockets. Then, even more carefully, transfer the pizza to the oven to bake for 15 to 20 minutes. Serve hot.

PUDDINGS

Upside-Down Honey and Walnut Pie

This recipe is frankly sinful and, to be honest, should have no place in this book. Just a glance at the list of ingredients will confirm the folly. The only crumb of comfort(!) that I can offer is, because it is rich, serve it in smallish portions with the merest dribble of cream!

Pastry
150 g (5 oz) 85% plain brown flour
75 g (3 oz) vegetable margarine

Caramel
100 g (3½ oz) light, soft brown sugar

Filling
75 g (3 oz) light, soft brown sugar
4 size 2 eggs
120 ml (4 fl oz) clear honey
3 tablespoons melted margarine
½ teaspoon natural vanilla essence
200 g (7 oz) chopped walnuts

MAKES 16 SLICES

Heat the oven to 170°C (325°F/Mark 3).

You will need a round, sloping-sided pie tin, 4 cm (1½ in) deep, base 18 cm (7 in), top 24 cm (9½ in). Do not grease the tin and, please note, do not attempt this recipe in anything other than a tin because liquid caramel has to be poured into the base.

Prepare the pastry by rubbing the fat into the flour. Use about 1½ tablespoons cold water to combine the mixture to a firm unsticky dough. Wrap in cling-film and chill for about 1 hour.

Now make the caramel. Have ready by the stove the warmed pie tin and a cup of cold water. Gently heat the sugar and water until all the sugar is dissolved, then boil briskly for about 2 minutes. The caramel stage has been reached when a drop of it sets firm immediately on contact with the cold water. Test constantly as the caramel boils. As soon as the caramel has reached the right stage *instantly* remove the pan from the heat and pour the caramel into the pie tin and tilt to coat the base with caramel. Leave to become firm.

In a bowl combine the remaining sugar, eggs, honey, melted margarine and vanilla. Beat well to mix, then stir in the chopped walnuts. Pour into the pie tin on top of the caramel.

Roll out the chilled dough to a round just slightly larger than the top of the tin – about 25.5 cm (10 in). Transfer the dough to cover the pie allowing it to fall down onto the filling, then press the dough firmly to the rim. There should be little or no need to trim any pastry from the rim.

Bake in the centre of the oven on a baking sheet for about 1 hour. Remove and leave for 5 minutes. Run a knife around the inside edge of the pie, trimming off the rim. Invert onto a plate and leave until warm before serving with single cream.

Honey and Nut Pie

A real 'wholefoody' sort of pie, best served warm or cold with thick pouring cream or with a thin apricot purée. To do this I soak 225 g (8 oz) apricots; use half for the recipe as instructed and thin the remainder with additional soaking liquor to serve as a sauce.

Pastry
225 g (8 oz) 100% plain wholewheat flour
100 ml (4 fl oz) vegetable oil
3 tablespoons cold water

Filling
110 g (4 oz) unsulphured dried apricots
240 ml (8 fl oz) clear honey
50 g (2 oz) vegetable margarine
¼ teaspoon ground cloves
1 teaspoon cinnamon
3 eggs
110 g (4 oz) rolled oats
110 g (4 oz) mixed, chopped nuts (any kind
　　except peanuts)
juice of 1 lemon

SERVES 6-8

Put a baking sheet to heat in the oven at 180°C (350°F/Mark 4).

Use a round, sloping-sided pie tin measuring 4 cm (1½ in) deep, base 18 cm (7 in), top 24 cm (9½ in). Grease lightly. (Note: This is exactly the right size tin for this recipe. Choose a slightly larger baking tin if necessary, but nothing smaller, or you will have filling left over.)

Put the flour in a mixing bowl. Combine the oil and water together in a measuring jug and with a fork, beat until milky. Add to the flour and mix to a dough. Transfer the dough to the baking tin and using your fingers press it into an even lining, bringing the pastry up the side slightly higher than the tin and crimping with thumb and forefinger to form an attractive edge.

In a separate bowl leave the dried apricots to soften in just sufficient boiling water to cover whilst preparing the rest of the filling.

Measure the honey into the mixing bowl you made the pastry in, (save on washing up!) and beat in the margarine until thoroughly combined. Add the spices, then beat in the eggs, one at a time, beating well between each addition. Finally, stir in the oats and nuts.

Drain the apricots, reserving their soaking liquor. Reduce them to a thick, but spreadable, purée in a food processor or liquidizer, thinning first with lemon juice, then a little soaking liquor if necessary. Make the flavour sharp to contrast with the honey and nut filling. Spread in the base of the pastry-lined tin and pour the honey/nut filling on top. Bake on the heated baking sheet in the centre of the oven for 1 hour. This recipe will not rise during baking, but when ready it should be browned and a metal skewer inserted into the centre of the pie will come out clean. Serve warm.

Alternative Christmas Pudding

1 egg
150 g (5 oz) dark, soft brown sugar
3 tablespoons vegetable oil
grated rind of 1 orange
110 g (4 oz) grated carrots
200 g (7 oz) grated potatoes
1 teaspoon bicarbonate of soda
150 g (5 oz) 100% plain wholewheat flour
2 tablespoons wheatgerm
1 teaspoon cinnamon
good pinch of ground cloves
150 g (5 oz) sultanas
75 g (3 oz) currants
50 g (2 oz) chopped walnuts   SERVES 6-8

Liberally grease a 1½-litre (3-pint) heatproof pudding basin.

Beat the egg in a large mixing bowl; add the sugar and continue to beat until paler in colour. Stir in the oil and remaining ingredients. Mix thoroughly before spooning into the greased pudding basin. Cover with a greased and pleated sheet of greaseproof paper followed by a pleated sheet of foil. Make the covering watertight by tying string tightly around the rim of the bowl. Cook in a saucepan of gently boiling water covered with a well-fitting lid for 3 hours. Turn out onto a warmed serving dish and serve with hot custard or creamed smetana.

Apple and Fresh Ginger Crumble Cake

There is definitely something about the flavour of fresh ginger that makes it worthwhile using, and nowadays it is not too hard to buy. If you are unable to get it in your area, substitute 1 teaspoon dried ginger. Pears or fresh peaches can be substituted for the apple filling.

Crumble
110 g (4 oz) 100% plain wholewheat flour
110 g (4 oz) fine oatmeal
50 g (2 oz) wheatgerm
110 g (4 oz) light, soft brown sugar
2 teaspoons peeled and freshly grated root ginger
¼ teaspoon bicarbonate of soda
¼ teaspoon cream of tartar
150 g (5 oz) vegetable margarine

Filling
275-350 g (10-12 oz) cooking apples
1 teaspoon lemon juice

SERVES 6

Heat the oven to 180°C (350°F/Mark 4).
Grease a shallow, 20-cm (8-in) round sandwich tin.
Put all the dry ingredients in a mixing bowl. Rub in the margarine to give a rather irregular crumb mix. Put half in the prepared tin and smooth it flat with the back of a spoon.
Quarter, core and peel the apples. Slice them, about 3 mm (⅛ in) thick, into a bowl containing the lemon juice, tossing the slices as you work. Arrange these in the tin in concentric circles, slightly overlapping one slice with another. Sprinkle the remaining crumble on top and bake in the centre of the oven for 45 minutes. Serve warm or cold with single cream.

Rhubarb and Ginger Pudding

Moist and not too sweet; a real pudding that cries out to be served with custard.

450 g (1 lb) trimmed rhubarb
275 g (10 oz) 100% plain wholewheat flour
2 teaspoons dried ginger
1 teaspoon bicarbonate of soda
110 g (4 oz) vegetable margarine
150 ml (¼ pint) clear honey
115 ml (4 fl oz) buttermilk

SERVES 6

Heat the oven to 180°C (350°F/Mark 4).
Liberally grease a deep, 23-cm (9-in) round cake tin.
Cut the trimmed rhubarb into 1-cm (½-in) slices. Combine the flour, ginger and

bicarbonate of soda in a bowl. Rub in the margarine until the mixture resembles coarse breadcrumbs.

Measure the honey into a measuring jug and pour the buttermilk on top. Whisk together with a fork and pour onto the dry ingredients. Stir just enough to combine and no more. Spread about a third of this mixture onto the base of the tin. Cover with half the rhubarb. Spoon another third of the mixture over the surface and spread out. It will by no means cover the rhubarb and will look highly irregular, but do not worry. Cover with the remaining rhubarb and finish with the last of the pudding mixture. Tap the tin on the work surface to settle the ingredients.

Bake in the centre of the oven for 1½ hours. After 40 minutes cover loosely with a sheet of foil. Serve hot or warm with home-made custard.

Plum and Raisin Oat Crumble

If this is cut into squares and served warm it can be served as a pudding. Served cold, cut into bars, it can be offered as a cake.

Filling
450 g (1 lb) plums, quartered and pitted
50 g (2 oz) raisins
2 tablespoons 100% semolina
1 tablespoon light, soft brown sugar
2 teaspoons cinnamon

Crumble
175 g (6 oz) 85% plain brown flour
150 g (5 oz) rolled oats
150 g (5 oz) light, soft brown sugar
75 g (3 oz) wheatgerm
1 teaspoon baking powder
225 g (8 oz) vegetable margarine   MAKES 24 BARS OR 12 SQUARES

Heat the oven to 180°C (350°F/Mark 4).

Grease a shallow rectangular tin, 27 × 16.5 × 3 cm (10½ × 6½ × 1¼ in).

Prepare the filling by tossing all the ingredients together in a bowl until thoroughly mixed.

The crumble is almost as simple. Put the dry ingredients together in a bowl and rub in the margarine to give a lumpy crumble mixture. Spoon half of it into the greased tin and use the back of the spoon to even and flatten it out. Spread the plum mixture on top and cover with the remaining crumble mixture. Bake in the centre of the oven for 45 minutes, or until tinged with brown and feeling fairly firm. Cut into bars or squares when it has cooled for 15 minutes.

Linzer Torte with Fresh Raspberries

This is traditionally made using raspberry jam but I much prefer the sharpness of the fresh fruit.

Almond pastry
75 g (3 oz) vegetable margarine
75 g (3 oz) light, soft brown sugar
grated rind of 1 lemon
good pinch of ground cloves
¼ teaspoon freshly grated nutmeg
75 g (3 oz) 100% plain wholewheat flour
about 110 g (4 oz) whole almonds, finely
  ground

Filling
350 g (12 oz) fresh raspberries

SERVES 6-8

You will need a 23- to 24-cm (9- to 9½-in) enamel pie plate.

To make the almond pastry, beat together the margarine and sugar with the lemon rind and spices. Work in the flour and about 75 g (3 oz) of the finely ground almonds, or sufficient to bring the mix together to form a dough that leaves the side of the bowl clean. Form into a ball, wrap in cling film and refrigerate for about 1 hour.

Heat the oven to 170°C (325°F/Mark 3) and place a baking sheet in it.

Reserve slightly less than a third of the dough. Pat out the rest on the plate. Scatter the base with the remaining almonds and top with about half the raspberries. Roll small pieces of the reserved dough into thin pencil-sized lengths. Lay these strips end to end to create a lattice-work effect, three strips one way and three the other. Bake in the centre of the oven for 50 minutes or until the pastry looks browned and cooked. Remove from the oven and push the remaining fresh raspberries between the lattice-work of the pie. Serve warm or cold.

Sharp Apple Crumble Pie with Nut Crust

Don't be tempted to sweeten the apples, no matter how sour, it is not necessary in this recipe.

Base
110 g (4 oz) ground walnuts, hazelnuts or
  almonds
175 g (6 oz) 100% plain wholewheat flour
75 g (3 oz) dark, soft brown sugar
grated rind of 1 lemon
75 g (3 oz) vegetable margarine

Topping
75 g (3 oz) 100% plain wholewheat flour
75 g (3 oz) rolled oats
50 g (2 oz) dark, soft brown sugar
2 teaspoons mixed spice
75 g (3 oz) vegetable margarine

Filling
450 g (1 lb) cooking apples

MAKES 12 SLICES

Heat the oven to 190°C (375°F/Mark 5).

You will need a 25.5-cm (10-in) round, 2.5-cm (1-in) deep, flan tin.

Put the dry ingredients for the base in a bowl and rub in the brown sugar so no lumps remain. Melt the margarine and pour into the mixture. Stir until the mix comes to resemble a coarse crumble. Press the crumble mixture around the base and side of the tin and bake on a baking sheet in the centre of the oven for 20 minutes.

While the nut crust is baking combine all the ingredients for the topping. Rub in the fat until this too forms a coarse crumble. Grate the apples, skin and all, onto a plate.

Sprinkle sufficient oatmeal crumble into the nut crust just to cover the base. Spread the grated apple on top, then top with the remaining crumble. Cover loosely with foil and return to the oven to bake on a baking sheet for 30 minutes. Remove the foil and bake for a further 10 to 15 minutes. Serve warm or cold.

Carob and Walnut Pudding

This is one of those strange puddings where a sauce is poured over the creamed mixture and miraculously they change places during baking to give a light sponge topping over a sauce at the bottom of the baking dish. This is then topped with meringue. As always, cocoa powder can be used instead of carob.

Sponge
110 g (4 oz) vegetable margarine
110 g (4 oz) dark, soft brown sugar
2 egg yolks
110 g (4 oz) 100% plain wholewheat flour
1 teaspoon baking powder
3 tablespoons carob or cocoa powder
50 g (2 oz) chopped walnuts
about 150 ml (¼ pint) skimmed milk

Meringue
2 egg whites
75 g (3 oz) dark, soft brown sugar

Sauce
50 g (2 oz) dark, soft brown sugar
40 g (1½ oz) carob powder
275 ml (½ pint) boiling water

SERVES 5-6

Heat the oven to 180°C (350°F/Mark 4).

Grease a deep, 1½-litre (3-pint) ovenproof baking dish.

In a bowl cream the margarine and sugar together until paler in colour. Beat in the egg yolks one at a time. Fold in the flour and baking powder with a little of the measured milk. Sift in the carob and add the walnuts. Fold in the remaining milk or sufficient to give a soft consistency. Spread in the prepared dish.

In a separate bowl combine the sugar for the sauce with the sieved carob. Gradually blend in the boiling water to form a smooth thin paste. Pour over the base and bake in the centre of the oven for 45 minutes.

Meanwhile, put the egg whites in a grease-free bowl. Whisk until stiff but not dry, then gradually whisk in the sugar. Spread the meringue over the pudding and return to the oven. Reduce the oven temperature to 150°C (300°F/Mark 2) for a further 45 minutes. Serve warm.

Fresh Cranberry and Orange Pie with Wheatgerm and Flake Crust

A lovely pudding for an autumn Sunday lunch.

Crumb crust
175 g (6 oz) wheat flake cereal with 30% bran
25 g (1 oz) wheatgerm
75 g (3 oz) vegetable margarine
1 tablespoon honey

Filling
3 eggs
110 g (4 oz) light, soft brown sugar
50 g (2 oz) vegetable margarine
3 tablespoons thawed, concentrated orange juice
50 g (20 g) 85% plain brown flour
225 g (8 oz) fresh cranberries, chopped
25 g (1 oz) chopped nuts   MAKES 12 SLICES

Heat the oven to 190°C (375°F/Mark 5).

Use a round, sloping-sided pie tin, measuring 4 cm (1½ in) deep, base 18 cm (7 in), top 24 cm (9½ in). It is not necessary to grease the tin. This tin is exactly the right size for the recipe. If you use a smaller tin the filling will certainly overflow – so use a larger pie tin if you haven't one the right size.

To make the crumb crust put the wheat flakes into a plastic bag and crush with a rolling pin until the flakes are reduced to a fine crumb. Empty into a bowl and mix with the wheatgerm. Warm the margarine and honey together in a small saucepan and combine with the wheaty mixture. Press the crumbs evenly into the pie tin using the back of a spoon. Pay special attention to bringing the crumb mix up as high around the edge as possible. Bake in the centre of the oven for 5 minutes, then remove and leave to cool.

For the filling, separate the eggs, placing the whites in a large, clean, grease-free bowl and the yolks in a separate mixing bowl. First whisk the egg whites until stiff but not dry. Gradually whisk in 50 g (2 oz) of the measured sugar and keep whisking until the whites form a stiff meringue. Add the remaining sugar to the egg yolks with the margarine and orange juice. Beat well and when thoroughly mixed beat in the flour. Stir in the chopped cranberries and a heaped tablespoon of the beaten egg whites. Fold in the remaining egg whites and spoon into the crumb crust. Sprinkle with the chopped nuts and return to the oven to bake at the same temperature for 15 minutes. Reduce the heat to 170°C (325°F/Mark 3) and bake for a further 45 to 50 minutes until browned, risen and firm in the centre. Serve hot or cold.

Lemon Meringue Pie – Blender Fashion

I include this recipe not because it is quick or easy to make, but because of the flavour which results from using a blender for making the filling. Liquidizing the whole lemons imparts what is to me a lovely, slight bitterness to the filling, somewhat reminiscent of my grandmother's marmalade puddings I ate as a child.

Pastry

175 g (6 oz) 85% plain brown flour
50 g (2 oz) 100% semolina
50 g (2 oz) finely ground nuts (almonds,
    hazelnuts or walnuts)
75 g (3 oz) vegetable margarine
1 tablespoon honey
2 tablespoons water

Filling

3 egg yolks
2 large lemons
50 g (2 oz) cornflour
425 ml (¾ pint) water
6-7 tablespoons clear honey
1 tablespoon vegetable margarine

Meringue

3 egg whites
75 g (3 oz) Demerara sugar   SERVES 6-8

Heat the oven to 200°C (400°F/Mark 6). Put a baking sheet on the centre shelf of the oven.

Have ready a 24- to 25.5-cm (9½- to 10-in) fluted flan ring.

To make the pastry, put all the ingredients together in a bowl and stir until they come together to form a non-sticky dough that leaves the side of the bowl clean. Roll out and use to line the flan ring. Do not worry if the pastry cracks or there are shortfalls in some areas; simply cut and patch wherever necessary, smooth the patched bits over with the back of a spoon and it will soon look immaculate. Prick the base all over with a fork and bake on the baking sheet in the oven for 15 minutes. Remove when baked and reduce oven temperature to 180°C (350°F/Mark 4).

Meanwhile, prepare the filling. Scrub the lemons, quarter and cut each quarter in half. Put in the liquidizer goblet with the egg yolks, cornflour and 275 ml (½ pint) of the measured water. (The full 425 ml (¾ pint) is too much for most liquidizers to take.) Blend briefly for about 10 seconds. Position a nylon sieve over a saucepan and pour the contents of the goblet into it. Using a wooden spoon firmly press all the juices from the pulp; discard the pulp. Add the remaining 150 ml (¼ pint) water and bring to the boil, stirring. Boil gently for 3 minutes, then remove the pan from the heat. Stir in honey to taste; it should not need more than 7 tablespoons as it is much better kept quite sharp. Dot the surface with the flakes of margarine and leave until warm.

Beat the filling briefly, then spread in the pastry case. Whisk the egg whites in a large grease-free bowl until stiff but not dry. Gradually whisk in the sugar, sprinkling it onto the meringue a tablespoonful at a time. Continue whisking until the sugar granules have all but dissolved and the meringue forms stiff, high peaks. Spoon over the surface of the filling, then spread carefully to cover the filling, making sure pastry and meringue meet all round the edge. Return to the oven to bake on the baking sheet, in the centre of the oven for 30 minutes or until the meringue is golden. Serve warm or cold.

Lemon Meringue Bread Pudding

This is a close relative of Queen of Puddings, but cutting down on the usual amount of sugar.

2 tablespoons vegetable margarine
425 ml (¾ pint) skimmed milk
50 g (2 oz) light, soft brown sugar
75 g (3 oz) fresh wholemeal breadcrumbs
3 eggs, separated
grated rind and juice of 1 large lemon
1 tablespoon light, soft brown sugar   SERVES 4-6

Heat the oven to 180°C (350°F/Mark 4).

Use about 1 teaspoon of the margarine to grease an 845-ml (1½-pint) ovenproof deep pie or soufflé dish.

Pour the milk into a saucepan and heat until it steams. Remove from the heat and stir in the breadcrumbs. Cover and leave aside.

Put the remaining margarine in a bowl and beat together with the sugar, egg yolks and grated lemon rind. Add the breadcrumb mixture, stirring briskly. Pour the mixture into the greased dish. Bake in the centre of the oven for 30 to 35 minutes when the breadcrumb mix should have set firm.

Five minutes before the cooking time is up have the egg white ready in a large grease-free bowl. Whisk until stiff, then gradually whisk in 1 tablespoon sugar and beat until silky. Carry on whisking whilst gradually adding the juice of the lemon. Spread this over the breadcrumb base, then return the pudding to cook for a further 15 minutes or until the meringue is golden brown. Serve hot.

Apple Roll with Cider Sauce

A good family pud! It is made Swiss-roll style, then sliced, and a cider syrup poured over before baking. It can be served with custard, but I like a thin, rather tart apple purée served with it. A good way of using up a surplus of windfalls!

Roll
110 g (4 oz) 100% plain wholewheat flour
110 g (4 oz) 85% plain brown flour
4 teaspoons baking powder
4 tablespoons vegetable margarine
7-8 tablespoons skimmed milk

Syrup
55 ml (2 fl oz) honey
75 ml (3 fl oz) dry cider

Filling
2 medium-sized cooking apples
2 tablespoons dark, soft brown sugar
1 teaspoon cinnamon

MAKES 11 SLICES

Heat the oven to 180°C (350°F/Mark 4).

Liberally grease a deep, 23-cm (9-in) round cake tin.

Put the flours and baking powder into a bowl. Rub in the margarine until uniformly incorporated. Add sufficient milk to combine into a soft dough.

Turn out onto a floured surface, knead briefly and roll out to a rectangle 30 × 23 cm (12 × 9 in). Quarter, core and peel the apples, then slice very thinly. Sprinkle the surface of the dough with the sugar, cinnamon and apples. Roll up from one long side. Slice into 11 rounds (a funny number, but this is what fits best in the tin). Arrange the slices, cut side down in the tin, eight around the outside edge, three in the centre. Measure the honey into a measuring jug and make up to 150 ml (¼ pint) with cider. Pour this over the apple slices and bake in the centre of the oven for 30 to 35 minutes. Serve warm.

One-Stage Minted Blackcurrant Bake

This recipe is very straightforward and quick. Blackberries can be substituted but they do not have the delicious tartness of blackcurrants. Miss out the mint if fresh cannot be had, the dried version is only a pale shadow of the fresh herb.

225 g (8 oz) blackcurrants, stalks removed
150 g (5 oz) 100% plain wholewheat flour
150 g (5 oz) 85% plain brown flour
225 g (8 oz) light, soft brown sugar
2 teaspoons baking powder
150 ml (¼ pint) vegetable oil
150 ml (¼ pint) skimmed milk
2 eggs
3 tablespoons chopped fresh mint

SERVES 8

Heat the oven to 180°C (350°F/Mark 4).

Liberally grease a sloping-sided roasting tin, base measurement 18 × 24 cm (7 × 9½ in). Run flour around the interior of the pan and tip out the excess.

Put all the ingredients into a mixing bowl, except for the blackcurrants. Beat thoroughly to combine, then transfer to the prepared tin. Sprinkle the blackcurrants over the surface and transfer to the centre of the oven to bake for 1½ to 1¾ hours, or until risen and firm in the centre. Serve warm with cream.

Grapefruit Pudding Cake

One of those border-line ones again – is it a pudding, is it a cake? I think this one just makes it into the pudding class.

275 g (10 oz) light, soft brown sugar
150 g (5 oz) 100% plain wholewheat flour
150 g (5 oz) 85% plain brown flour
110 g (4 oz) vegetable margarine
½ teaspoon ground allspice
grated rind of 1 orange
150 ml (¼ pint) buttermilk
1 egg
1 teaspoon bicarbonate of soda
1 grapefruit
110 g (4 oz) mixed, chopped nuts and seeds (for
  example hazelnuts, sesame and poppy seeds)   MAKES 12-16 SLICES

Heat the oven to 180°C (350°F/Mark 4).

Liberally grease a deep, round cake tin with a removable base, 20 to 21.5 cm (8 to 8½ in) in diameter.

Put the first six ingredients into a mixing bowl, then rub in the margarine until the mixture resembles fine breadcrumbs. Sprinkle half the crumbs (about 370 g (13 oz)) into the prepared tin. Put the buttermilk in a bowl, add the egg and bicarbonate of soda and whisk together to combine thoroughly. Stir into the remaining crumb mix in the bowl. Peel and chop the grapefruit into small pieces, discarding all the pips. Add this, with any juices, to the mixture, stir, then spoon into the cake tin. Process or blend the combined nuts and seeds to a fine meal and sprinkle over the pudding mixture. Transfer to the centre of the oven to bake for 1½ to 1¾ hours, or until the cake is firm in the centre and shows signs of shrinkage from the side of the tin. Leave for 10 minutes before running a knife around the edge and removing from the tin. Serve warm with creamed smetana or yogurt.

Fruit Baked with a Hazelnut Scone Crust

Although I have used 450 g (1 lb) of dried fruits in this recipe at least double the quantity of seasonal fresh fruit can be substituted: rhubarb, apple and blackberries, plums and peaches for example. As always, try to use the minimum of sugar to sweeten.

Filling
450 g (1 lb) dried, mixed fruit
570 ml (1 pint) apple juice or cider
2 teaspoons lemon juice

Scone topping
110 g (4 oz) 85% plain brown flour
2 tablespoons wheatgerm
1 tablespoon light, soft brown sugar
1 teaspoon baking powder
½ teaspoon bicarbonate of soda
3 tablespoons vegetable margarine
50 g (2 oz) toasted, chopped hazelnuts
4 tablespoons yogurt
1 tablespoon skimmed milk
1 tablespoon Demerara sugar

The night before put 425 ml (¾ pint) of the apple juice or cider in a saucepan with the dried fruit. Bring to the boil, then cover and simmer gently for 10 minutes. Remove the pan from the heat and leave overnight. The following day add the remaining apple juice or cider and the lemon juice. Pour the fruit and juice into a 1½-litre (3-pint) deep baking dish.

Heat the oven to 220°C (425°F/Mark 7).

Put the flour, wheatgerm, sugar, baking powder and bicarbonate of soda into a bowl. Rub in the fat until the mixture resembles fine breadcrumbs. Mix in the toasted, chopped hazelnuts. Combine the yogurt and milk together and stir into the mixture to form a soft dough. Turn out onto a lightly floured work surface. Roll out to a rectangle about 1 cm (½ in) thick. Cut the dough into strips 3 to 4 cm (1¼ to 1½ in) wide, then cut each strip across diagonally to form diamond shapes. Use about 12 diamonds, overlapping them on top of the fruit round the edge of the dish. Sprinkle the Demerara sugar over the scone dough and bake in the top third of the oven for 15 minutes. At this stage move the dish to the lowest third of the oven, lay a sheet of foil over the top and reduce the oven temperature to 180°C (350°F/Mark 4). Continue baking for a further 30 to 45 minutes or until the fruit is tender when tested with a fork. Serve warm with single cream.

Soft Berry Shortcake

Beautifully simple, this can be made from a combination of the first or last berries of the season, when there are precious few to be had. In other words you an use just one type of fruit or a combination of any of the following: red, black and white currants, strawberries, raspberries, loganberries.

225 g (8 oz) berries, prepared as appropriate
1 rounded tablespoon light, soft brown sugar
110 g (4 oz) 85% plain brown flour
½ teaspoon baking powder
60 g (2½ oz) light, soft brown sugar
40 g (1½ oz) vegetable margarine   MAKES 8 SLICES

Heat the oven to 180°C (350°F/Mark 4).

Grease a round, shallow sandwich tin, 20 cm (8 in) in diameter. Sprinkle the berries in the base, quartering strawberries, if used.

Measure the remaining ingredients into a bowl; rub in the margarine until the mixture resembles fine breadcrumbs. Sprinkle the mixture over the fruit, then press it down lightly with a fork.

Bake in the centre of the oven for 25 minutes. Serve warm, cut into wedges, with a little *fromage frais*.

Blackberry and Apple Slump

This is derived from a traditional American recipe. As to the origin of the word 'slump' I do not know, but the dish is basically a fruit stew with dumplings. I have used blackberry and apple but the type of fruit can be just about anything you choose. Eat fresh and hot with chilled smetana or soured cream.

700 g (1½ lb) cooking apples
450 g (1 lb) blackberries, washed and picked
  over
about 2 tablespoons Demerara sugar

Topping
1 tablespoon Demerara sugar
1 teaspoon ground cinnamon

Dumpling mix
225 g (8 oz) 85% plain brown flour
4 teaspoons baking powder
1 tablespoon vegetable margarine
150 ml (¼ pint) skimmed milk   SERVES 5-6

Select a large saucepan, 21.5 to 23 cm (8½ to 9 in) in diameter, with a well-fitting lid.

Quarter, core and peel the apples. Slice into the saucepan, then put the blackberries in on top. Cover and cook over a very low heat for 30 minutes. Gently stir in sufficient sugar to taste.

In a bowl combine the flour and baking powder. Rub in the fat. Stir to form a soft dough with the milk. Take heaped teaspoonfuls of the mixture and drop onto the surface of the barely simmering fruit. Combine the sugar and cinnamon and sprinkle a little of this topping mixture over each dumpling. Re-cover and continue to simmer very gently for 15 to 20 minutes. Serve piping hot.

Up-Market Bread Pudding

Good hot or cold and would grace the table of a dinner party!

275 ml (½ pint) dry cider
225 g (8 oz) dried prunes
110 g (4 oz) dried apricots
150 ml (¼ pint) skimmed milk
110 g (4 oz) wholewheat bread, crusts removed
25 g (1 oz) vegetable margarine
110 g (4 oz) Demerara sugar
grated rind of 1 orange
3 tablespoons Calvados or rum
2 tablespoons mixed poppy and sesame seeds   SERVES 6

The previous day bring the cider, prunes and apricots to the boil. Simmer gently, covered, for 10 minutes, then cover and leave overnight.

The following day heat the oven to 190°C (375°F/Mark 5).

Liberally grease a 1½-litre (3-pint) deep baking dish.

Re-heat the prunes and apricots. Cook covered until almost all the liquid has been evaporated or absorbed. Remove from the heat. Measure the milk into a bowl and crumble in the bread. Meanwhile add the rest of the ingredients except the poppy and sesame seeds to the saucepan in the order given. Lastly stir in the soaked bread. Pour into the baking dish, sprinkle with the seeds and bake in the centre of the oven for 1 hour. The pudding will be slightly risen and cooked through in the centre (dig a spoon in and take a look if you are not quite sure). Serve warm or cold.

Apple and Pear Soufflé

A very humble-sounding dish but it has an excellent flavour.

4 egg yolks
75 g (3 oz) light, soft brown sugar
2 tablespoons 85% plain brown flour
275 ml (½ pint) skimmed milk
½ teaspoon natural vanilla essence
2 small cooking apples
2 teaspoons lemon juice
2 very ripe pears
1-2 tablespoons Calvados or gin
up to 1 tablespoon brown sugar
5 egg whites   SERVES 5-6

You will need a 1½-litre (3-pint) soufflé dish, or deep baking dish; grease well.

If you have a food processor or liquidizer combine the first five ingredients and blend until smooth, or, combine ingredients in a bowl and whisk until smoothly blended. Pour into a saucepan and heat, stirring constantly. When the mixture boils remove the pan from the heat. (Do not worry about the egg yolks curdling, the presence of the flour in the sauce will prevent this.) Cover and leave to cool.

Heat the oven to 180°C (350°F/Mark 4).

Quarter, core and peel the apples. Slice into a small saucepan, add the lemon juice, cover and cook over a very low heat until reduced to a pulp. Remove from the heat. Quarter, core and peel the pears. Chop roughly before stirring into the apple pulp. Mash these together with a potato masher (unorthodox, but it has the desired effect). Add the spirit, taste and sweeten if desired, then cover and leave on one side.

Have the egg whites ready in a clean, grease-free mixing bowl. Whisk until stiff, but not dry. Position a nylon sieve over the egg whites and rub the cooled sauce through the sieve. (This takes care of any skin that may have formed.) Fold the two together carefully, using a large metal spoon, keeping as much air in the mixture as possible. Put half this in the base of the soufflé dish, then spread with the apple and pear mixture. Top with the remaining soufflé mixture and spread flat. Using your thumb or a knife mark a circle in the mixture, about 4 cm (1½ in) from the rim of the dish.

Bake in the centre of the oven for about 45 minutes. At this stage it will probably be not quite set in the centre. If you prefer it a little more cooked, give it another 10 minutes, but, as with most soufflés, it is best served just a little on the creamy side.

DOWN TO THE LAST CRUMB

Fish Pie with Green Herb Crust

It is the herb crust that makes this recipe special. Here it tops a fish and vegetable mixture. This is only one idea of the many different ways it can be used, topping a whole variety of goods with the herbs adapted to the flavour of the other ingredients and according to season (because they definitely need to be fresh herbs).

Herb crust

75 g (3 oz) wholewheat breadcrumbs
50 g (2 oz) freshly grated Parmesan cheese
50 g (2 oz) grated Gruyère cheese
3 tablespoons chopped fresh parsley
3 tablespoons chopped watercress leaves
3 tablespoons chopped celery leaves
grated rind of 1 lemon
freshly ground black pepper

SERVES 4

Fish mixture

450 g (1 lb) smoked haddock on the bone
570 ml (1 pint) skimmed milk
1 tablespoon vegetable oil
2 rashers unsmoked lean back bacon
1 onion, chopped
2 sticks celery, diced
350 g (12 oz) cubed potatoes
1 green pepper, de-seeded and diced
2 teaspoons cornflour mixed to a paste with 1
    tablespoon white wine, cider or water
110 g (4 oz) sweetcorn kernels

This dish can be served in individual 570-ml (1-pint) fireproof casseroles or in one of 2¼-litre (4-pint) capacity.

The herb topping is very easy, simply toss everything together in a bowl.

Put the fish in a fish kettle or frying pan and pour in the milk. Bring to simmering point, then remove from the heat, cover and leave aside for 5 minutes. Drain the fish reserving the poaching liquor. Separate the fish from all the bones and skin reserving the flaked fish in a bowl.

In a large saucepan heat the oil and the rinds from the bacon. Slice the bacon across into strips and fry in the oil for a minute or two before stirring in the onion and celery. Cover and cook gently for 5 minutes, then add the potatoes and green pepper and cook for a further 5 minutes. Remove the bacon rinds before pouring in the reserved poaching liquor from the fish. Cook gently, uncovered, until the vegetables are just tender. Turn up the heat and stir in the cornflour paste. Bring to the boil, stirring gently, and then allow to simmer for 2 to 3 minutes. Stir in the flaked fish and sweetcorn kernels, heat through, then taste and season with freshly ground black pepper (I doubt whether any salt will be necessary.) Ladle the fish mixture into the casserole(s) and fork the crumb crust over the top. Grill until the topping looks well browned and crunchy. Serve piping hot with a crisp green salad tossed with a really lemony dressing.

Cheese and Herb Sausages

110 g (4 oz) fresh breadcrumbs
4 small spring onions, trimmed and finely
    chopped
a handful of parsley sprigs, finely chopped
1 teaspoon fresh thyme leaves, finely chopped
1 teaspoon English mustard powder
salt and freshly ground black pepper
150 g (5 oz) grated mild cheese e.g.,
    Lancashire, Cheshire
1 egg yolk mixed with 1-2 tablespoons milk

Coating
50-75 g (2-3 oz) fine, dry breadcrumbs or
    oatmeal
vegetable oil, for frying
1 egg white, lightly beaten   MAKES 12

If you have a food processor put the lumps of bread, the onions, herbs and seasonings together and process until fine. Lightly fork in the cheese, and, just as lightly, bind with the egg yolk and milk.

Or, combine the ingredients together in a bowl in the order given. Bind with the egg yolk and milk treating the mixture lightly and avoiding compressing it into a solid, dense lump. Gently form the mixture into a ball and divide into 12 equal portions. Form into little sausage shapes. Dip in the lightly beaten egg white and roll in crumbs or oatmeal. Fry gently in a little vegetable oil until browned. Drain on kitchen paper and serve hot.

Wholewheat Macaroni Bake

A good family supper dish.

275 ml (½ pint) hot skimmed milk
50 g (2 oz) fresh brown breadcrumbs
110 g (4 oz) wholewheat macaroni
1-2 tablespoons vegetable oil
1 onion, chopped
1 green pepper, de-seeded and chopped
1 packet (about 75 g (3 oz)) watercress,
  chopped

175 g (6 oz) Cheddar cheese, grated
4 tablespoons yogurt
2 eggs, beaten
salt and freshly ground black pepper
3 medium-sized tomatoes
2 tablespoons grated Parmesan cheese

SERVES 4-6

Heat the oven to 180°C (350°F/Mark 4).

Pour the hot milk into a bowl and stir in the breadcrumbs. Leave aside to soak for several minutes.

Read the packet instructions for cooking the macaroni and boil in salted water for rather less than the time advised so the pasta is just tender, not soft. Drain thoroughly in a colander, then stir into the breadcrumbs and milk.

Heat the oil in a pan and gently fry the onion and pepper until softened but not browned. Add this also to the breadcrumb mixture with the chopped watercress, Cheddar cheese, yogurt and beaten eggs. Stir well, then taste and season with a little salt and freshly ground black pepper. Pour the mixture into a greased 1-litre (2-pint) ovenproof casserole. Slice the tomatoes and arrange on top of the macaroni mixture. Sprinkle with the Parmesan, then transfer to the oven to bake for about 1 hour or until set firm in the centre. Serve hot with salad.

Pappa Al Pomodoro

A dish my sister had in Florence and has raved about ever since. As with all ostensibly 'simple' dishes it relies on top quality ingredients.

800 g (1¾ lb) tomatoes, peeled and chopped
4-5 tablespoons olive oil
1 leek, trimmed, washed and finely chopped
½ very small dried chilli
1 teaspoon tomato purée
8 fresh basil leaves, chopped
1½ litres (3 pints) good home-made chicken
   stock
salt and freshly ground black pepper
500 g (generous 1 lb) home-made wholewheat
   bread.

For serving
1-2 tablespoons olive oil
1-2 tablespoons grated Parmesan cheese

SERVES 4-6

Heat the oil in a large saucepan. Stir in the leek and chilli. Cover and cook gently without browning for 10 minutes. Stir in the tomato purée, followed by the tomatoes and basil. Stir, bring to a simmer and simmer for 5 minutes. Now add the stock and a little salt and freshly ground black pepper. When it comes to the boil, crumble in the bread. Stir and simmer gently for 2 minutes. Cover and cook for 1 hour. Eat hot, tepid or cold with a little fresh olive oil stirred in and a scattering of freshly grated Parmesan.

Caesar Salad

Again, a fairly simple recipe but the ingredients need to be top quality and the preparation impeccable if the salad is to succeed. This is a salad I prefer to eat with my fingers but I don't for one moment assume that you will join me on the downhill path!

2 cloves garlic, cut into slivers
150 ml (¼ pint) olive oil
2 large Cos lettuces
175 g (6 oz) small button mushrooms
juice of 1 large lemon
2 large eggs, at room temperature
sea salt and freshly ground black pepper

¼ teaspoon Worcestershire sauce
4 slices wholewheat bread from a large loaf,
   sliced ½ cm (¼ in) thick and cubed
6 tablespoons freshly grated Parmesan cheese

Marinade the garlic in the oil for at least 2 hours. Strain the oil.

   Separate the lettuce leaves and select the inner unblemished leaves. Wash them if you feel you must, I prefer not to. Dry meticulously with kitchen paper then roll up in a clean teatowel and store at the bottom of the refrigerator until ready to serve. Wipe the mushrooms with damp kitchen paper and slice thinly. Toss thoroughly with lemon juice.

Bring a pan of water to the boil and add the eggs. Boil for 1 minute only and remove.

In a small bowl combine ½ teaspoon salt with the Worcester sauce and freshly ground black pepper. Add the lemon juice drained from the mushrooms and 6 tablespoons of the garlic-flavoured oil to make a dressing.

Heat the remaining oil in a frying pan and fry the cubed bread, turning constantly until an even golden brown. Drain on kitchen paper.

Dress the salad just before serving. Place the lettuce leaves in a large salad bowl. I prefer to leave them whole, but tear them into large pieces if you like. Pour over the dressing and use your hands to turn the leaves in it. Break the eggs into the centre and turn again. Now sprinkle in the mushrooms and Parmesan. Turn again and coat thoroughly. Serve immediately, sprinkled with the garlic croutons.

Bobotie

A slightly unusual South African dish, that has a lightly curried meat base and a savoury, lemon-flavoured egg custard top. To make it is very easy, to spell it is something else!

2 tablespoons oil

1 large onion, chopped

450 g (1 lb) good-quality, lean minced beef or
    lamb

50 g (2 oz) chopped almonds

50 g (2 oz) sultanas

1 large cooking apple, cored and chopped

2 teaspoons hot curry powder

½ teaspoon turmeric

½ teaspoon ground cumin

1 tablespoon home-made chutney

generous squeeze of lemon juice

salt and freshly ground black pepper

1 (50-75-g (2-3-oz)) slice crustless wholewheat
    bread, about 3 days old

Topping

275 ml (½ pint) skimmed milk

grated rind of ½ lemon

2 size 2 eggs

SERVES 4-5

Heat the oven to 170°C (325°F/Mark 3).

Heat the oil in a medium-sized saucepan. Lightly brown the onion, then add the meat, a small batch at a time. When it is all browned add the almonds, sultanas and apple, then the spices, flavourings and seasonings. Stir well, cover and leave to cook gently.

Soak the bread in the measured milk and squeeze out the excess, back into the bowl. Crumble the bread into the meat mixture and mix well. Taste and season if necessary. Transfer the mixture to a deep, ovenproof dish and level the top of the mixture with the back of a spoon.

Add the grated lemon rind to the remaining milk and beat in the eggs. Season lightly and pour the topping over the meat mixture. Bake in the centre of the oven for 1 hour or until the topping has set. Serve hot.

Mozzarella in Carrozza

Italy's answer to the French *croque monsieur* – a delicious snack!

Cut slices of bread about ½ cm (¼ in) thick. If you want to make them look good, say, as a starter for a supper party, trim the bread to neat rectangles. Mostly the Italians do not seem to bother and leave the crusts on. Cut the mozzarella no thicker than the bread and trim to fit. Form into sandwiches, including an anchovy fillet in each one, if liked. Press firmly together.

Beat together 2 large eggs with some seasoning and pour onto a plate. Sit the sandwiches in the beaten egg, turning them from time to time to ensure they soak up as much egg as possible. Heat enough olive oil in a frying pan to come half-way up the sandwiches. If it looks as though there will be any difficulty in the sandwiches holding together, spear each one with a couple of toothpicks. Fry on both sides until golden. They are done when the mozzarella starts to escape! Drain on kitchen paper and serve piping hot.

Better Bread Sauce

You may not feel that such a simple dish warrants a recipe, but I have quite often been compelled to eat bread sauce that was so bad it was scarcely fit to hang wallpaper! Here is a better bread sauce . . .

425 ml (¾ pint) skimmed milk
1 medium-sized onion, stuck with 2 or 3 cloves
1 bayleaf
blade of mace
1 clove garlic, left whole

about 75 g (3 oz) not-too-fine breadcrumbs, made from 2-to-3-day-old home-made bread
25 g (1 oz) butter
2 tablespoons cream (optional)
salt and freshly ground black pepper

Put the first five ingredients into a saucepan. If you are fortunate enough to have an Aga or something similar, you can leave the covered pan at the back of the stove and forget about it for about 2 hours. Otherwise, bring the milk to just below boiling point as slowly as possible, the object being to gain the maximum infusion of flavours into the milk. This done, remove the flavouring ingredients and stir in the breadcrumbs. Leave for up to 2 hours, gently heating, to give the bread time to absorb the milk. Add the butter and cream and season with salt and freshly ground black pepper to taste. Consistency is a debatable point. It will vary according to the type and age of the bread used, but in the end it is a matter of personal taste. I think it should be thick enough just to hold its shape when a spoonful is served on a plate, but others prefer it poultice-thick!

Note Some people like to chop the soft onion and replace it in the sauce before serving.

Royal Rarebit

As this is such a good standby recipe, I usually make it in fairly large quantities. This recipe is sufficient for eight large slices of toast so you probably will not need all of it at once. If this is so, refrigerate whatever is left in a sealed container. It will form a firm paste which can be spread straight onto toast and grilled. The mixture will keep for up to a week.

275 ml (½ pint) dry white wine or cider
1 clove garlic, crushed
350 g (12 oz) Cheddar cheese, grated
2 tablespoons wholewheat flour
good pinch of cayenne pepper
freshly grated nutmeg
freshly ground black pepper

1 tablespoon good-quality Dijon mustard
2 teaspoons Worcestershire sauce
8 large slices home-made wholewheat bread, about 1 cm (½ in) thick
butter for spreading (optional)

Pour the wine into a medium-sized, heavy-based saucepan. Add the crushed garlic clove and bring to the boil. Turn the heat down to a simmer and leave uncovered to evaporate for 2 to 3 minutes.

Meanwhile put the grated cheese, flour, cayenne pepper and nutmeg in a large bowl. Season generously with freshly ground black pepper and toss together thoroughly. Add a handful of this mixture at a time to the just-simmering wine, stirring all the while with a wooden spoon. When all the cheese mixture has been added allow it to come up to the boil and bubble briefly, then switch off the heat. Stir in the mustard and Worcestershire sauce, then taste and season further as desired.

Toast as many pieces of bread as required, crusts removed, if you prefer; whether you then butter the toast is also a matter of choice. Arrange the toast on a fireproof serving dish (or plates) and pour on the cheese sauce. Replace under the grill and leave until browned and bubbling. Serve piping hot.

Hot Orange and Lemon Soufflé with Whisky

This is based on a recipe by one of my favourite cooks, Michael Smith.

2 large oranges
4 tablespoons whisky
juice of 1 large lemon
75 g (3 oz) dryish sponge cake crumbs
60 g (2½ oz) 85% plain brown flour
75 g (3 oz) light, soft brown sugar

275 ml (½ pint) skimmed milk
25 g (1 oz) vegetable margarine
4 egg yolks
5 egg whites

SERVES 5-6

Heat the oven to 200°C (400°F/Mark 6). Put a baking sheet in the oven to heat.

Liberally grease a 1½-litre (2-pint) soufflé dish, or deep, ovenproof dish.

Grate the orange rind and reserve. Peel the oranges with a sharp knife removing all the pith and membrane, then cut between the membranes of each segment in order to remove the whole orange segment, entirely free of pith or membrane. Put the segments in a bowl with any orange juice, and add a tablespoon of whisky and the juice of half the lemon. Toss with the cake crumbs and leave aside.

Put the flour and sugar in a medium-sized saucepan, stir to mix, then graduallly add the milk to obtain a smooth, thin paste. Heat the mixture, stirring constantly, until it forms a thickish paste. Remove from the heat and beat in the margarine, orange rind, remaining whisky and lemon juice. Beat in the egg yolks one by one.

Have the whites ready in a large grease-free mixing bowl. Whisk until they form stiff peaks. Stir about a third of this into the orange sauce, then carefully fold in the rest. Spoon half the mixture into the soufflé dish and cover with the orange and crumb mixture. Top with the remaining soufflé mixture, then transfer to the centre of the oven to bake on the baking sheet for 45 minutes. Serve immediately.

Wholefood Crumb Crust with Orange-Flavoured Apple and Meringue

Crumb crust
110 g (4 oz) dry cake, biscuit or breadcrumbs
50 g (2 oz) rolled oats
50 g (2 oz) hazelnuts, walnuts or almonds
25 g (1 oz) sesame seeds
4 tablespoons wheatgerm
50 g (2 oz) vegetable margarine
2 tablespoons clear honey

Filling
450 g (1 lb) cooking apples
rind of 1 orange
juice of ½ orange
about 1 teaspoon brown sugar
3 egg yolks
110 g (4 oz) dates, finely chopped

Meringue
3 egg whites
1 tablespoon light, soft brown sugar
juice of ½ orange
1 tablespoon Demerara sugar

MAKES 12 SLICES

Heat the oven to 180°C (350°F/Mark 4).

You will need a round, sloping-sided pie tin, 4 cm (1½ in) deep, base 18 cm (7 in), top 24 cm (9½ in). Put a baking sheet to heat in the oven.

To make the crumb crust put the first five ingredients into a food processor and process to obtain an even crumb. Combine the margarine and honey together in a medium-sized saucepan and heat gently until the fat has melted. Add the crumb mixture and stir well. Press this mix evenly around the base and side of the pie tin. Bake in the centre of the oven for 15 minutes.

Meanwhile, quarter, core, peel and thinly slice the apples into a saucepan containing all the rind but only half the juice of the orange. Cover and cook over a low heat for about 15 minutes or until the apples are reduced to a pulp. Taste and add the minimum amount of sugar; a teaspoonful should suffice. Beat in the egg yolks.

Sprinkle the chopped dates in the base of the crumb crust and spread the apple mixture on top. Return to the oven to bake for a further 15 minutes. Towards the end of this cooking time start preparing the meringue. Have the egg whites ready in a clean, grease-free bowl. Whisk until stiff, then gradually whisk in the tablespoon of sugar and continue beating until the meringue is silky. Carry on whisking, now gradually incorporating the orange juice. Spread the meringue over the pudding and sprinkle with the Demerara sugar. Return it to the oven to bake for a final 10 to 15 minutes or until golden brown. Serve warm or cold. (If kept longer than 24 hours the meringue tends to become a bit rubbery.)

Breadcrumb Griddle Scones

175 g (6 oz) fine dry wholewheat breadcrumbs
350 ml (12 fl oz) skimmed milk
1 tablespoon clear honey
1 tablespoon oil
1 egg
75 g (3 oz) 85% plain brown flour
2 tablespoons baking powder   MAKES 16-18

Combine the breadcrumbs and milk in a bowl and leave to soak for 15 minutes.

In a separate bowl whisk together the honey, oil and egg.

Place the flour and baking powder in a large bowl. Pour in the honey and egg mixture and stir to form a thick paste. Gradually spoon in the soaked breadcrumbs and milk to give a thick smooth batter.

Heat the griddle or frying pan and wipe with a wad of kitchen paper moistened with oil. Drop large spoonfuls of batter onto the griddle and leave until air bubbles appear in the mixture and the tops begin to look set. Use a palette knife to flip the scones over. Serve hot with butter and marmalade or honey for breakfast or with sour cream and damson cheese as a pudding.

Honey Tart

Not sweet or sickly at all.

Pastry
110 g (4 oz) Basic Wholewheat Shortcrust
  Pastry (see page 58)

Filling
75 g (3 oz) fresh wholewheat breadcrumbs
25 g (1 oz) vegetable margarine
150 ml (¼ pint) clear honey
1 teaspoon ground ginger
grated rind of 1 lemon
juice of ½ lemon

SERVES 6-8

Heat the oven to 200°C (400°F/Mark 6).

Put a heavy baking sheet to heat in the oven.

You will need an enamel pie plate 23 to 24 cm (9 to 9½ in) in diameter. Roll out the pastry and use to line the pie plate. Trim the excess pastry from the edge, then crimp the pastry rim between thumb and forefinger.

To make the filling combine all the ingredients together in a bowl and mix well before spreading in the pastry-lined case. Bake on the baking sheet in the centre of the oven for 25 to 30 minutes. Serve warm.

Honey and Breadcrumb Biscuits

These are really good, crunchy biscuits with the merest hint of spice.

110 g (4 oz) vegetable margarine
110 g (4 oz) dark, soft brown sugar
1 tablespoon honey
110 g (4 oz) fine, dry wholewheat breadcrumbs
110 g (4 oz) 100% plain wholewheat flour
½ teaspoon baking powder
½ teaspoon ground allspice
rolled oats for coating   MAKES 24

Heat the oven to 180°C (350°F/Mark 4).
   Grease two baking sheets.
   Put the margarine, sugar and honey together in a bowl. Beat until paler in colour. Add the breadcrumbs, flour, baking powder and allspice and work together until the mixture forms a dough. Roll into walnut-sized balls, coat in the oats and place on the greased baking sheets, allowing about 4 cm (1½ in) spreading space between biscuits. Bake in the centre of the oven for 25 to 30 minutes, or until the biscuits just feel firm in the centre. Leave to cool on the baking sheet for a few minutes before using a palette knife to remove to a wire rack. When cool, store in an airtight container.

Fruited Steamed Pudding

Very moist, but light even so, thanks to the breadcrumbs.

50 g (2 oz) large raisins
110 g (4 oz) vegetable margarine
110 g (4 oz) dark, soft brown sugar
2 eggs
50 g (2 oz) 85% self-raising brown flour
110 g (4 oz) wholewheat breadcrumbs

220 ml (7 fl oz) cooked, unsweetened fruit
   pulp, e.g., apples, plums, rhubarb
1 teaspoon bicarbonate of soda

SERVES 6-8

Liberally grease a 1- to 1½-litre (2- to 2½-pint) heatproof pudding basin. Squash the raisins into the base.
   In a separate bowl beat the margarine and sugar until paler in colour. Beat in one of the eggs. Fold in the flour, then whisk the remaining egg separately before folding into the mixture, followed by the breadcrumbs and fruit pulp. Mix the bicarbonate of soda with a tablespoon of water before stirring this in also. It will look a somewhat odd mixture but do not worry. Spoon it into the prepared basin and cover with a greased and pleated sheet of greaseproof paper. Cover this with a sheet of pleated foil and secure tightly with string around the rim of the bowl. Cook in a saucepan of gently boiling water, covered with a lid, for 2 hours. Turn out onto a warmed serving dish and serve with additional fruit pulp or custard.

Bakewell-Style Tart

If I called this just straightforward 'Bakewell Tart' the purists would shoot me down in flames! In this recipe you can mix ground almonds, cake or breadcrumbs in any ratio you like, or exclude the ground almonds altogether, nobody will ever know.

Pastry

175 g (6 oz) Basic Wholewheat Shortcrust
   Pastry (see page 58)
6 tablespoons no-sugar red jam

Filling

110 g (4 oz) vegetable margarine
110 g (4 oz) dark, soft brown sugar
2 eggs
½ teaspoon natural almond essence
150 g (5 oz) any combination of cake or bread
   crumbs and ground almonds
75 g (3 oz) 85% self-raising brown flour
2-3 tablespoons skimmed milk   SERVES 8

Heat the oven to 220°C (425°F/Mark 7). Put a baking sheet in the oven to heat.

Have ready a round, fluted, shallow tart tin, base measurement 23 cm (9 in) and 2.5 cm (1 in) deep.

Roll out the pastry and use to line the tin. Trim the excess from the rim and reserve all the pastry scraps. Spoon in the jam and spread evenly in the base.

In a mixing bowl beat together the margarine and sugar until paler in colour. Beat in one egg, followed by the almond extract. In a separate bowl whisk the remaining egg until foamy. Toss together the crumbs and flour, then fold the beaten egg and crumb mixture alternately into the creamed mixture. Lastly fold in the milk to give a soft dropping consistency. (The quantity of milk needed will depend on the type and dryness of crumbs used.) Spread this over the jam base. Re-roll the pastry trimmings to a band 23 cm (9 in) long and cut ½-cm (¼-in)-wide strips. Lay these in a lattice-work pattern over the filling. Transfer to the oven to bake on the baking sheet in the centre of the oven for 15 minutes. Reduce the heat to 180°C (350°F/Mark 4) and cook for a further 15 minutes or until gently risen and firm in the centre. Serve warm with thin pouring cream.

Note No-sugar 'jams' and fruit spreads are now available in many supermarkets as well as healthfood shops.

Conversion Tables

All these are *approximate* conversions, which have been rounded either up or down. In a few recipes it has been necessary to modify them very slightly.

OVEN TEMPERATURES

Mark 1	275°F	140°C
2	300	150
3	325	170
4	350	180
5	375	190
6	400	200
7	425	220
8	450	230

VOLUME

2 fl oz	55 ml
3 fl oz	75
5 fl oz (¼ pint)	150
½ pint	275
¾ pint	425
1 pint	570
1¾ pints	1 litre
(2 pint basin =	1 litre)

MEASUREMENTS

⅛ in	3 mm
¼ in	½ cm
½	1
¾	2
1	2.5
1¼	3
1½	4
1¾	4.5
2	5
3	7.5
4	10
5	13
6	15
7	18
8	20
9	23
10	25.5
11	28
12	30

WEIGHTS

½ oz	10g (grams)
1	25
1½	40
2	50
2½	60
3	75
4	110
4½	125
5	150
6	175
7	200
8	225
9	250
10	275
12	350
1 lb	450
1½	700
2	900
3	1kg 350g

Index